CAPITALISM IS BROKEN!

We need to fix it!

ROY WELLS

DEDICATION

Dedicated to my wonderful wife Lori and Uncle Roy.

Table of Contents

FOREWORD – WHAT IS TRUTH?

When I wrote this book, I wanted to make sure that my statements were supported by facts. I wanted to get to the truth. I remember watching the debates between Hillary Clinton and Donald Trump. Several times Clinton referred to 'fact checks'. (1) But what is a fact? What is the truth? How can we know what is true? This is a big problem with so many different claims made on the Internet.

Plato was a philosopher who lived in antiquity between 427 and 347 B.C.E. (2) He proposed the thought experiment that we know as the Allegory of the Cave. We don't respond to reality. We respond to our perception of reality. We are trapped in a cave that only shows us pictures of what is outside. (3) We have no way to compare our pictures with what is outside the cave. This is worse in the age of media. We can't personally verify the claims we hear. We are expected to believe that what the media says is true. We only hear what they tell us. But we can't verify for ourselves unless we travel to the place where the events happened. Even then, we would have to believe the witnesses and sources we met at the site. Before the Internet, media consisted of newspapers and broadcast TV news reports. These sources were heavily edited, and publishing was limited by gatekeepers. I recall hearing that journalists were committed to reporting the facts without bias. Journalists would tie every statement to sources and editors would check the facts. I'm not sure if anyone can report without bias. We all have biases, even if we don't want to admit them. But I recall that the news reporters tried to limit their biases. Today, people post whatever comes to mind. There are no editors or fact checkers on social media. Now we are flooded with claims and statements that have no basis in reality. You may have heard of 'alternative facts'. (4) There is no such thing. We all share the same facts based in reality. But how can we know them?

What is a fact? One example is something you can verify yourself through experience. Look at gravity. If you drop this book, it will fall. This is something you can try yourself. It's a fact that Joe Biden was president in 2023. Every source supports that claim and there are no credible sources that contradict that statement. Donald Trump passed a tax cut in 2017. (5) The standard deduction that could be used to reduce taxes was almost doubled for each type of filer from 2016 to 2017. (6) That's a fact. For my tax situation, I began using the standard exemptions because those were larger than what I could itemize. I saved money with the new tax laws. I claim it as a fact because I experienced it first-hand. You may notice that you saved money on taxes. The minimum wage was last raised in 2009 fifteen years ago. (7) This is a fact. Inflation is cooling down. (8) Jerome Powell, head of the Federal Reserve is the one who raised the interest rates to combat inflation. (9) Jerome Powell was sworn in during Donald Trump's administration in 2018. Then he was reappointed during Joe Biden's administration in 2022. (10) These are facts. Joe Biden reduced the number of leases for oil drilling on federal lands. That's on the public record. (11) Government statistics can be considered facts. The interpretations are a matter of opinion. Tesla claims that you can charge an electric vehicle battery from 20% to 80% in approximately 20 minutes. (12) It is likely a fact that it won't take less time. It is likely to take more time. You can fill a gas tank in less than five minutes. I know this because I timed it. If you check your time at the pump, you will probably find that to be true. If I say that you can tax the wealthy to pay for more government jobs, that is more of a researched opinion. I can't guarantee that I am right. I can only support my statements with facts. I can say that we tax the wealthy less now than we have in the past. (6) I can also say that there are fewer government jobs per person. Any statement after that is a conclusion. My collection of facts is very complicated. No political party has all the answers.

How do you know a statement is true? You can never truly know. The first step is to consider the source. Is the source reliable? I tend to trust Time, government sites, National Public Radio (NPR), CBS, NBC, ABC, Associated Press (AP), and Investopedia. I am more skeptical of Wikipedia because they have no central editing team. If I have never heard of an organization before, I tend to be skeptical. If it is on social media, I check the trusted sources. If something is on social media and I can't find it on a trusted news outlet, I assume I am dealing with fake news. If something is true, it tends to be repeated on multiple trusted news outlets. If I can't find it on a source I trust, I don't believe it. I won't use it as a source. Sometimes, I choose what I find to be more likely. I may read what certain 'experts' think and then look at it to be sure it makes sense. I tend to follow Robert Reich. It seems logical to me that if you give money to someone at the lower end of the economic spectrum, they will use that money locally to buy things from local businesses. It's logical to me that if you give money to someone in the 1%, you can't guarantee that they will invest that money or that they will spend it in this country. It is my opinion that society would do better to take a bottom-up approach than a trickle-down approach. It is my opinion that the rich are still getting richer, and the poor are still getting poorer. But that opinion is supported by data I have collected. The data I found suggests that financial inequality has grown in the last 40 years.

How can you tell if something you read may be credible? Get details. If a person posts something, they should be able to back it up with facts. If I read that the Democrats are causing businesses to fail with excess regulations, I want to know more. What regulations? If an article says that raising the minimum wage will burden businesses, I respond that we need to pay people fairly. If an article references a carbon tax, I want to know who benefits from collecting the money. If the article mentions nonsense fees to line someone's pockets, I think we should cut those fees. If no detail is given, I just ignore the article. Before I react to a statement, I want to know how the person came to their conclusion. I treat every claim with skepticism.

I think it is good to explore the scientific method. (13) First, you make an observation. Gather data to support that observation and reach a conclusion. Gather more data to confirm that conclusion. Publish your findings for informed peers to review. If your findings can be confirmed by your peers, then it can be called a theory. Our collection of knowledge consists of observations that have been observed, reviewed, tested, and confirmed by peers. If a scientific claim is untestable, then it is junk science. If a claim can't be backed up with data, it's just junk.

We may never know the whole truth. As our collection of knowledge increases, we know more of the truth. But our body of knowledge is constantly growing and changing. It is not the truth that changes. It is our knowledge of the truth that changes. So, our beliefs will change as we discover more of the truth. I am writing the truth as I see it.

I have reviewed data collected by the government, previous legislation, papers and articles on history, books on economics, and political articles. My findings had many nuances. No political party has all the answers. Sometimes, both political parties have it wrong. Neither side has the entire truth. The truth is somewhere in between.

CHAPTER ONE

CAPITALISM IS BROKEN!

CHAPTER ONE

CAPITALISM IS BROKEN!

Capitalism is broken. But I probably don't have to tell you that. Just look around. Years ago, we had the American Dream. The belief that if we work hard, we can succeed and achieve! A dream where we can have enough to live a comfortable life, own a home, and provide a better life for our children. (1,2,3) But for most of us, this is only a dream and not our reality. Whether it's runaway inflation, stagnant wages, mountains of student debt, bosses playing foolish games, or just ever-increasing bills; our reality has become a nightmare. Many of us must stitch together several jobs and side hustles to keep from being evicted. It is likely that we will work until we drop dead at our jobs!

According to a report by the Economic Policy Institute, wages adjusted for inflation have fallen for the lowest paid workers in the last 40 years. (4) Wages for middle class workers have been stagnant for the last 40 years while the pay for those at the top have skyrocketed. Productivity has risen but not purchasing power. We are working harder for less money! We are facing a generational crisis. My father managed to have a good paying job, a house, and a family at the age of 24 with only a high school diploma. I earned a bachelor's degree, and I was not able to purchase a house until I was 33. I never had children. This is just one example of the decline of the middle class.

Meanwhile, the richest man in the world has $200 billion dollars. (5) $200 billion dollars! How fair is that? If we divide that number by $1 million, we would have enough for 200,000 people to live comfortably in retirement. With $200 billion, we could buy nice homes for 1 million families. And yet the middle class is getting squeezed into poverty while the 1% could fill several swimming pools with all their money.

What are we going to do? It seems that those in charge always want to fill their pockets at the expense of everyone else. Should we abolish all property and have the government in charge? Can the government take care of everyone and distribute the wealth fairly? Or would those in charge just hoard the wealth? How can we make it worth it to work? Do you feel like those in charge are looking out for you? These are questions that civilization has been trying to solve for thousands of years. Sometimes, the people have made progress. The American Revolution, the Golden Age of Capitalism, and the rise of the unions are good examples. The Golden Age of Capitalism is considered to have happened between 1940 and 1970. During the Golden Age of Capitalism, workers were paid fairly, our infrastructure was built, and the future looked bright. The government provided many good paying jobs to stimulate the economy. But as soon as the pressure was off, those in charge found a way to profit from our sweat and labor. Now we are suffering from neoliberalism and trickle-down economics that don't seem to be trickling down. Our jobs are going to China and Mexico. Neither the Republicans nor the Democrats are truly looking after our livelihoods and interests. We haven't raised the minimum wage in fifteen years. The wealthy often pay a lower percentage of taxes than the 99%. How can we make lasting change? In the chapters throughout this book, we are going to explore the history and pitfalls of capitalism. Then we will learn about possible solutions and how we can take back our future!

CHAPTER TWO

———

COMMUNISM & SOCIALISM

CHAPTER TWO

COMMUNISM & SOCIALISM

Wouldn't it be nice if we had our government work together to take care of us? Perhaps you dream of having the government select a career for you. In this dream, the government would provide a nice home for you and your family in exchange for your time, skills, and labor. Perhaps the government might also provide a pension for after you have reached a certain age. It's understandable that we would want some agency to look after us to make sure everything is fair. This is the dream of the socialist society. This may explain why so many people support Bernie Sanders. Forty six percent of people polled by USA Today had a favorable view of Sanders. That's higher than Biden and Trump received in the same survey. (1) One 2019 poll in AXIOS found that 61 percent of Americans between the ages of 18 and 24 had a positive reaction to socialism. (2) In 2020, Bernie Sanders almost won the Democratic Party nomination for president of the United States. Sanders once declared, "I am a socialist and everyone knows it." (3) Who wouldn't want the government to erase their debt and redistribute the wealth? Think of how many homes could be bought with the money that the 1% is hoarding. Before we commit, we should take a long look at socialism and communism.

What is Socialism and Communism?

Socialism is where the government or workers own and control the means of production and wealth. (4) Communism is a system in which goods are owned in common and are available to all as needed. It also prohibits private property by definition. (5) Karl Marx, the father of communism, referred to socialism as a phase to introduce communism into an economic system. Socialism is different from communism in that communism does away with the concept of private property while socialism lets you keep your property. However, many communist countries call themselves socialist countries. It's important to keep definitions in mind. Many times, people will use terms incorrectly. Socialism can be a catch all phrase to mean many different things. Socialism can be used to describe systems that are communist as well as capitalist systems with strong social programs. For our purposes, it just means that the government or society owns the means of production.

Socialism and communism have many things in common. Let's start with communism. It's only fair that we look at the history of communism and see how this philosophy has worked for the people. There are five items to note.

1. Bourgeois and Proletarians (The Everlasting Class Struggle)
2. Proletarians and Communism (The 'People'/State Decide)
3. Absolute Loyalty to the State (Loyalty to State over all)
4. Abolition of Property! (No Private Property)
5. Possibility of Revolution (VIOLENCE!)

Bourgeois and Proletarians (The Everlasting Class Struggle)

According to Marx, you have the bourgeois (bor.zhwaa) and the proletarians. (6, Marx, pages 14, 15) The bourgeois represent the elite while the proletarians represent the common workers. These groups represent the two classes that have been battling for thousands of years since the dawn of civilization. The elites have constantly prospered from the labor of the workers. Before the Industrial Age, you would have a few groups that would not be part of this struggle. Those outside might be artists and craftsmen. Today, they may represent the self-employed businesspeople.

During the Middle Ages, most people fell into three classes. People were either a lord, a merchant/craftsman, or a peasant. Peasants or serfs worked the land for their lord. They would be responsible for providing a certain amount of crops to their lord. Incidentally, this is where we get the term landlord. During this time, the serfs were considered property of the landlord. If the land was sold, the ownership of the serfs changed too. While the planting and harvesting season would have you working from sunup to sundown, there were multiple holidays and seasons where you didn't have to work as much. Since the serfs couldn't acquire property, they only worked to produce what was needed.

With the dawn of the Industrial Age, it was normal for the workers to be pooled together to work for the owner of the factory. You can be sure that the elite owners would squeeze as much from the workers while giving as little in return. The Industrial Revolution ushered in a new form of oppression where the people were gathered in dirty cities to work long hours in dirty unsafe factories and then go home to live in crowded, dingy apartments with their entire family. Even young children had to work. Children who lived at the factory may have had to work eighteen-hour days. Often, children were maimed or killed in the unsafe factories. (7,8) The small, 'inefficient' workshops were replaced by big factories and many of the craftsmen were run out of business to work as laborers for low wages. It was also normal for big businesses to form monopolies or cartels so that they could price gouge the consumer for inferior goods. (9) I firmly believe that those in charge would have us go back to those days if it weren't for the laws that were made to keep the greedy in check.

Today, we have runaway inflation coupled with runaway corporate profits. Do we get a share of these profits? No! The minimum wage hasn't increased since 2009. (10) We have corporations tossing people into the streets with no thought to the damage that this does to communities. We have corporations sending jobs overseas. Are these overseas factories safe? We have investment bankers playing all sorts of illegal tricks on Wall Street while our hopes of retirement lie dashed on the rocks. (11) We have corporations scheming with 'legal' cons to fleece the working poor. (12) I think it is safe to say that those in charge are seeking to oppress us.

An alternative to the greedy business owners would be to have the State in charge. Rather than having separate corporations compete to provide goods and distribute wealth, it may make sense to have a central organization efficiently perform these services. According to Karl Marx, 'Each according to their ability. Each according to their needs.' In practice, the cream always rises to the top. One of the problems with communism and socialism is that you still have people at the top who are in control of the economy. How much do you trust the politicians to run your future?

The Power to the State (and Only to the State)

The goal of the Communist Party is to have the State in charge and ONLY the State. By definition, communism means ownership by the people, workers, or society. Many who mean well would emphasize that the workers could own the factories. As a rule, the communist governments have owned the property rather than the workers. In other words, you may exchange one greedy boss for another. The new boss will be the same as the old boss.

Even with socialism, the State owns most or all the institutions for producing wealth. Once again, you have the power of the economy in the hands of a few. With socialism, you can have a democratically elected government control the economy. While you can still own private property, your boss is still the State. Your only choice for services is the government. If you don't like the goods or services you receive, you don't have any other choice. Socialism lends itself to centralization.

Absolute Loyalty to the State (and Only to the State)

Another facet of communism is loyalty to the State above religion and even family. Karl Marx referred to religion as the 'opium of the people'. Any attachment over the State has not been tolerated in communist countries. Any churches that exist would have to have all activity approved by the State. (6, Marx, page 48) This assumes that churches are allowed to exist at all. (13) The State would even demand loyalty over your own family. In the Communist Manifesto, Marx lists a free public education as part of his program. With the free 'education', your children would be instructed and indoctrinated to be more loyal to the State than their own parents. (14) Perhaps the school will teach your children to turn you over to the authorities if you give any hint that you don't unconditionally support the current government. When the State controls all businesses and institutions, you do not have any other choices! You have no control over what the school teaches your kids.

Marxists want to raise your children and control your future, money, and career. In Marxism, the family is believed to be a unit where wives are oppressed by their husbands and children are oppressed by their parents. This oppression must be broken up and mothers must leave their homes and join the workforce. (15)

Marxism in practice is totalitarian. The term totalitarian was first used by supporters of fascist dictator Benito Mussolini, who summed it up this way: "Everything within the State, nothing outside the State, nothing against the State." (16)

According to Hannah Arendt, a totalitarian society is one in which the State seeks to displace all prior traditions and institutions, with the goal of bringing all aspects of society under control. A totalitarian state is one that seeks to completely define and control reality. Truth is what the rulers decide it is. (17) A perfect example is illustrated in George Orwell's book Nineteen Eighty-Four. (18)

Abolition of Property (No Private Property)

One of the primary end goals of Communism is to abolish private property. All goods would be common. What does that even mean? Many like to imagine a world where we have no possessions, no religion, and we live in brotherhood and harmony. What would it be like to have no property? This does not sound anything like the American Dream. Do you want the government to decide what property you can have? Do you want the government to decide your future with no hope of ever doing better?

Economist Iain Murray said, "The central issue with income inequality is that people who seem to be most concerned with it never really ask the question, how are the poor actually doing? Because when you asked that question and look at the data that answers it, you will see that the poor do the best in economically free societies and do the worst in societies where they are controlled in one way or another, whether it be by socialist, or fascist, or authoritarian regimes." (19)

Possibility of Revolution (Not a Commitment to Violence, Just Likely)

Marx wrote that he does not recommend violence and that he would be the first to discourage revolution. Really? I think he wrote this part to stay out of trouble. Historically, all Communist countries involved bloody and violent revolutions!

History of Communism

The hope is that you would have a benevolent organization that would determine where each person should work, then that organization would provide benefits accordingly. Since we have had several nations try this approach, I think it is only fair to see what has resulted. I will review the results based on freedom, standard of living, and level of violence. Several nations who have tried communism include Russia, Cuba, Venezuela, & China. Maybe their workers found that they were free from oppression.

Venezuela

Let's start with Venezuela. Before the oil crash in the 1980's, Venezuela was the wealthiest nation in South America. The per capita income rivaled the United States. The people enjoyed liberty, freedom, and economic opportunity. (20)

In 1988, the people elected Hugo Chavez as their president. Once in power, Chavez implemented the playbook of other communist nations. He rewrote the constitution. He provided free healthcare and free education through college. When the Supreme Court ruled against Chavez, he added more judges to 'pack the courts'. When he was reelected in 2006, he centralized the media and removed all voices of dissent. He authorized government agencies to seize private property for the citizens. He centralized all businesses. His final step was to eliminate term limits and set himself up to be president of Venezuela for life. (21)

When Chavez died in 2013, Nicolas Maduro took over. He went even further to enforce a Marxist agenda. As of 2022, Venezuela is now in crisis! More than seven million refugees have left the country seeking a better life. The country is now victim to hyperinflation, violence, and food & medicine shortages. Cholera, malaria, and malnutrition have returned. (22)

China

China is a contender for becoming the next superpower. But would you want to live there? China's Cultural Revolution led by Mao Zedong, was a brutal conflict that killed 40 to 80 million people. (23) While Marx states that he hoped to avoid violence in bringing about communism, massive violence seems to always be the method used to bring it about.

Most of the 1.3 billion citizens of China have no say in who runs the country. The ruling Communist Party picks its leaders every five years behind closed doors. (24) There is no representation for anyone outside the party. China has one of the worst records for human rights abuses. (25) Some of the issues include the right to health and adequate food, online censorship, and arbitrary arrest and detention. Women continue to endure sexual violence and harassment. There is no right of expression or freedom of religion. During the height of COVID, there were reports that some citizens had the doors to their homes welded shut so that they could not violate quarantine. (26) Many were left to scramble to figure out how they would feed themselves and their families. China is quickly becoming the country with the most surveillance of its citizens. (27) The city of Chongqing is estimated to have one camera for every 5.9

citizens. This is 30 times the rate you will see in Washington, D.C. Facial recognition software is used to catch criminals and even shame jaywalkers at busy intersections. Muslims in China are flagged if they let their beards grow too long. Big Brother is very much alive and well in China. (18) Surveillance in China has helped put an estimated 1 million people into "re-education centers" that are like concentration camps, according to the U.N. Many were arrested, tried, and convicted by a computer algorithm based on data harvested. In China, you can even be arrested for having a banned app on your phone. Not only must you avoid bad behavior, but you are also under constant pressure to act in ways that the party approves. You must constantly be active in your support of the party. Not only can you not openly criticize the government, but you must also be shown actively supporting the government. People are even required to use a registered ID just to rent a karaoke booth. China is now using Big Data and surveillance to start a Social Credit system to encourage 'positive behavior'. This system uses constant surveillance to assign points based on certain behaviors. Behaviors such as arguing with neighbors, jaywalking, or not cleaning up after your dog will cost you points. Positive behaviors such as reading propaganda (Study the Great Nation), volunteering, or donating blood will gain you points. If you don't have enough points, you will face real life consequences such as not being able to get a loan, job, or book high speed train tickets. Perhaps next China will analyze people's facial expressions for 'face crimes'. (18) Do you want to live in a society that scrutinizes your every move?

The job situation in China certainly isn't any better than it is in the United States. Many young people are giving up 16-hour days or fruitless job searches to move in with their parents to be full-time children. (28) The Chinese workforce appears to experience grueling work hours or a dismal job market. One worker stated, 'I lived like a walking corpse.' More than one in five between the ages of 16 and 24 are jobless. In America, job seekers over 50 will sometimes experience age discrimination. In China, they have the 'curse of 35'. Employers in China are less willing to hire workers older than 35 because the younger workers are cheaper. Many post social media pictures where they are 'lying flat' because they are disillusioned with studying hard to find that it doesn't pay.

China has been experimenting with 'state capitalism'. It seems that China manages to have the worst of both worlds where they exploit their workers and scrutinize their every move. At least Americans are free to disapprove of the government. China has started to allow certain companies (both foreign & domestic) to operate to make money. However, Communist philosophy trumps the free market. The capitalist companies in China had better toe the party line or else! This is known as party-state capitalism. One company to run afoul of the party line was Ant, run by Jack Ma. In the fall of 2020, Ant was about to sell shares in the largest initial public offering in history, but regulators abruptly suspended the IPO, and Ma disappeared for a while. It appears Ma made critical comments about the party's risk tolerance. Eventually, Ant had to restructure and pay a fine of $2.78 billion. This is an example that the Chinese Communist Party will squash any business if it feels the business will interfere with its programs. (29)

Cuba

Cuba had a rocky history even before Communism. In the 20th Century, Cuba had been plagued by corruption, violent overthrows, and economic uncertainty. When Fidel Castro began his campaign to rule Cuba, he started with violence, death threats to political candidates, and kidnapping. Castro's rule was secured by force. While Batista may have rigged the election that he won, Castro's rise to power fits with the communist principle of rule by force. (30)

After Castro rose to power, he began to implement policies such as expropriation and heavier taxation. Castro used the expropriation policy to confiscate real estate regardless of who owned it. Many American businesses lost their properties in Cuba. The US protested, but Castro declared that his decision was final. That's the real risk of investing in a country that is communist. You never know when the government will confiscate your property. I would not be surprised if China were to expropriate all the factories and business that our corporations built there.

According to a report from the U.S. State Department, Cuba has a poor human rights record. Among their issues include unlawful & arbitrary executions, civil rights abuses to dissidents and political prisoners, interference with privacy, censorship, threats of violence against the press, serious restrictions on internet freedom, freedom of speech and assembly, freedom of movement, and gender equality. (31) Like any other communist country, Cuba does not treat its citizens well.

Cuba's economy is often characterized as stagnant and troubled. Brain drain, where all the smartest residents leave, is also a problem. All the state institutions are in a state of decay, but things are unlikely to change due to the regime's stranglehold on the country. (32) Cuba is not known as a land of opportunity. As you can imagine, no one would want to invest, or stay, or work hard in a country like Cuba. While the embargos are partially responsible for the poor state of the Cuban economy, it is no surprise that the country can't flourish with random violence, restrictions, and expropriation.

Russia

Finally, we come to Russia. The flagship of Communist philosophy. The original Russian Revolution in 1917 was not characterized by the bloodshed that plagued other communist countries. Under Vladimir Lenin, it seemed that the proletariat utopia might finally be achieved. (33) It wasn't until Joseph Stalin took over that the mega-deaths began. Almost 1 million died in Stalin's bid to purge the Communist Party. Another 5 million died during the famine caused by Stalin's collectivism. (34) We must admit that before communism, life wasn't great in Russia. At the turn of the 20th century, Russia was a backwards country that was plagued by oppression and corruption. They entered the Industrial Revolution decades later than other countries. It seems that many countries turn to communism out of desperation. Rule by the people & communal sharing of resources sound good in theory. But in practice, you must worry about who rules the government. Lenin's rule started out to be an improvement until Stalin took over. It only takes one bad leader to send a country into oppression and ruin. The loss of our Freedom is only one election away.

At the beginning of the Russian Revolution, the peasants ran the landlords off their land. The peasants took control. The landlords had to flee to avoid being tortured and murdered. The Russian government officially declared that all lands would belong to the peasants that farmed them rather than to the landlords. The dream became a nightmare under Stalin. Stalin started with a five-year plan to rapidly industrialize the nation. He ruthlessly enforced targets that were impossible to reach. Those who failed to reach those targets were imprisoned or executed. Under Lenin, Soviet agriculture was mostly handled by small landowners. Stalin began collectivization under the state to address the inefficiencies in small scale farming. In retaliation, many of the farmers began killing livestock and hoarding grain. The resulting famine killed around 5 million. Stalin even had millions of small land holders killed or imprisoned. Stalin began a purge of the Communist Party where the people were encouraged to inform on one another. He established secret police to enforce his rule. Three million were imprisoned and almost one million were executed.

As you can imagine, human rights were dismal under Cold War Russia. Freedom of speech, free labor unions, private corporations and churches were not tolerated. Freedom of movement was also curtailed. Even private property was limited. (35) High ranking party members may be able to own houses and automobiles. Status, not wealth, determined citizens' living conditions. And that status could be revoked if you were found to be disloyal to the party. Andrey Vyshinsky was quoted as saying that rule of law & civil liberties were examples of 'bourgeois morality'. (36,37) While human rights have drastically improved since Stalin's rule, these conditions show the worst that Communism and centralism has to offer.

According to a report issued by the CIA, living standards in the USSR have always struggled to approach the standard held by the United States. (38) According to this report, housing, domestic property, and health care were meager compared to the United States. The report noted shortages in housing and health care. The only bright spot is that the Soviet diet was beginning to catch up to the food that was available in the United States.

Assessment of Communism

It seems that oppression is difficult to avoid. We feel that we are being oppressed in our current capitalist system. Often, countries faced oppression by their former governments before turning to communism. But history shows that communism is also oppressive by its nature and in practice. Communism has almost always been implemented by massive violence and bloodshed. But once in place, the bloodshed doesn't end. To stay in place, communism has a history of oppressing its people by arbitrary executions, suppression of basic human rights, and subjugation of the individual to the State. Accepting communism is akin to taking a vow of poverty. This is the problem with any attempt at centralization. Those at the top tend to have no regard for nor input from those they govern. You take what you get from the top and you had better like it or else! Communism promises equality, fairness, and brotherhood, but what it has delivered is far more sinister! We need to be careful that we don't become so desperate for change that we commit to making a horrible mistake. After reviewing communism, I advise that we try something else.

Socialism

While communism involves taking away personal property and total control by the State, perhaps socialism will provide a better solution. Socialism involves society or workers controlling the means of production. That is, they own the businesses. There is also the principle of collectivism. In collectivism, regulations are made that improve society. The economy is not just guided by naked self-interest with no regard for others. Let's look at socialism to see if that will work for the United States.

Differences from Communism

There are several differences between communism and socialism. Socialism allows you to keep private property. The best form of socialism would be the Nordic Model adopted by Sweden, Norway, Finland, Denmark, and Iceland. According to this model, only major corporations are run by the government. Small businesses can still operate. Socialism is expected to come about by regulation and not by bloodshed. In democratic socialism, human rights are generally respected. While the State is still in charge of most forms of production, the people elect their leaders in free elections. Strong labor unions help to manage the wages and benefits for the workers.

The Nordic countries have some elements of capitalism, so they are not strictly socialist. These countries do have a strong safety net for citizens. They do a better job of sharing societal risks. They provide services such as education, childcare and strong labor protections. Their success may be partly cultural. Their system has grown around a shared culture of trust and cooperation. However, these countries do have higher taxes. (39)

So then, what's wrong with socialism? Should we try it? One tenet of socialism is the concept that the individual should sacrifice for the common good. Stalin presented an extreme example where the State did not even consider the individual. Some countries such as Canada, the Scandinavian countries, or other European countries have a reputation for being cooperative. In America, we cherish our Individuality. If we were to adopt more socialist policies, we might have to sacrifice or change our identity as rugged individualists. We also cherish the many freedoms we have. We as Americans would not rush to give up our freedoms even if it was for the common good. Many believe that we have the right to endanger ourselves even if it risks higher costs to society. For instance, some believe we should have the right to not wear seat belts, even if the insurance companies must pay higher costs when we have more serious injuries in crashes. Even if it were better to sacrifice some personal freedoms for the greater good, that is not something all of us are willing to do. This is one reason that widespread socialism would be hard to adopt in the United States.

Centralism is another problem with socialism. The government would plan and run the businesses. How can a central board plan for an entire economy? With capitalism, each company is responsible for its own operations. Its leaders have a much smaller scope to view. If the company is not able to be profitable, then it will go out of business to be replaced by a more efficient company. With government supervision, a program or business can continue to run even if it is a waste of money. How can a central planning board keep in touch with the needs of the customers? How can a central planning board anticipate what the citizens want? How will minorities be considered if the central planning board is out of touch with certain members of its society? How can we be sure that there isn't corruption in the department that plans the business activity? Capitalist businesses are accountable to shareholders and customers. Who holds the planning board accountable?

If the State owns most of the corporations, then that must mean there are fewer corporations. The government wouldn't open two corporations to compete with itself. With fewer corporations, there are fewer companies offering jobs and perhaps fewer jobs in total. It is more likely that companies will conform to a specific mold. If you don't like the company where you work, you wouldn't have as many options for a new job.

When the state owns most of the corporations, there is also no competition and less choice. With competition, companies will operate efficiently and do everything possible to anticipate potential needs for new customers. We may oppress our workers, but you have endless choices for breakfast cereal to eat. But with a central planning board, how many new ideas will be produced? Workers aren't protected, but capitalism has produced an almost endless variety of new goods and services. A variety that would not be possible with only a few key people in charge.

Without the incentive to earn more, why should we work hard? Let me ask you this. What motivates you more? Making the world slightly better for your neighborhood or city? Or making more money so you can provide a better life for you and your family? If there is no link between effort and reward, then there is no incentive to work hard. Why should I work hard if there is no extra reward for doing a good job?

In 1841, Charles Ripley formed Brook Farm just a few miles from Boston. He sold shares to raise money. A share would get you membership and citizenship to his farm. You could choose to do any work that you wanted. Everyone made the same wage regardless of what they did. Everyone was equal. But what happens if one person is irresponsible? What happens if your coworker doesn't want to work hard? After three years, he decided to conform to the teachings of Charles Fourier because the farm was struggling. This included strict mandates and nightly lectures. Fourier directed that members be paid extra for certain jobs and that there would be levels to accommodations based on contribution. The farm built a grand building that they called a Phalanx. But shortly after completion, it burned to the ground. Many of the members were tired of the demands of the farm, so they left. The farm was completely closed by 1847. With strict collectivism, everyone shares in the benefits, but that sharing is in no way tied to the effort produced. There must be an incentive tied to working harder. (40)

Let's consider the tragedy of the commons published in an article by Garrett Hardin in 1968. This was in reference to a lecture by William Forster Lloyd. (42)

'Therein is the tragedy. Each man is locked into a system that compels him to increase his herd without limit — in a world that is limited. Ruin is the destination toward which all men rush, each pursuing his own best interest in a society that believes in the freedom of the commons.'

—Garrett Hardin, The Tragedy of the Commons (41)

In this tragedy, every man uses a common pasture to feed their animals. But who replenishes the field? Every man has an incentive to use the pasture without limit, but no one has the incentive to limit their use or replenish the pasture. Before long, the pasture loses all its grass because there is no incentive to take care of the pasture. Why maintain someone else's property?

We are probably stuck with capitalism. There are advantages to capitalism, but we must address the issues we face. I can't imagine that it is possible to have the government own corporations without a lot of restructuring. The disruption would be too painful for most of us to bear because it would likely affect our jobs. The transition would bring this country to its knees. We would have to tear down all the corporations and institutions then build new ones. The system is broken. People are angry. We need to fix the system before we lose it. People are so angry; they may accept any solution. We may become so angry that we will rush to a solution and make a huge mistake.

The final issue with socialism is that it leads to higher taxes. Socialist countries who follow the Nordic model have almost twice the amount of their GDP taxed than the United States. (39) Even in the most individualistic capitalist societies, we still need to have government programs. We need defense, roads & infrastructure, and programs to help people get on their feet again. But we need to be able to pay for this. This money comes from some place and there is a limit to what we can do. But what are we to do? We can't keep going with the level of oppression we are facing. It's not a fault that our economy has inequality. The fault is that there is so much inequality because corporations and the rich are making so much money at the expense of its workers. The rich are getting a free ride. Is this how capitalism was supposed to be?

CHAPTER THREE

CAPITALISM & DEMOCRACY

CHAPTER THREE

CAPITALISM & DEMOCRACY

Capitalism has been around since the dawn of civilization. Before there was currency, there was barter. Merchants from ancient civilizations would negotiate prices and trade for their goods or services. Capitalism just means that the means and ownership of production are in the hands of private parties and not the government. (1) Capitalism has been the preferred choice to run economies in Western Society since the demise of the feudal system. Unfortunately, this system did not always do much for the poor in previous centuries. This reminds me of some of the stories by Charles Dickens. In the 16th century, the wealthy were assumed to be more virtuous than the poor. Therefore, the poor deserved their miserable lot. There was no accounting for general misfortune.

Adam Smith is considered by many to be the father of modern capitalism. He influenced how the United States would implement capitalism when he published The Wealth of Nations in 1776. (2) Communism wouldn't be proposed until 1848. So, capitalism was the only option.

The 10th amendment of our Constitution reads, "The powers not delegated to the United States by the Constitution, nor prohibited by it to the States, are reserved to the States respectively, or to the people." (3) This can be taken to mean that decisions are meant to be resolved at the lowest level possible. The U.S. government was much smaller two centuries ago. Our government took a 'hands off' approach unless there was a crisis. This fits with laissez-faire capitalism where the government lets the economy run its course without interference. (4)

The world was much different 200 years ago. While corporations have been around for hundreds of years, they weren't like the colossal corporations we have today. All businesses would be considered small businesses by today's standards. These businesses would include small factories, stores, workshops, craftsmen, and farmers. (5,6)

Smith's writings were influenced by studying historical economic systems and the expansion of the North American colonies. He started by reviewing economic conditions that started after the fall of the Roman Empire in the west.

After the fall of the Roman Empire in the west, civilization was in chaos. For a short time, there was anarchy. But anarchy never lasts for long. Before long, the strong will naturally come together to form governments that benefit those at the top. Groups grow and absorb smaller groups until these groups become too big to fail. Without democracy, these groups become nations where the conditions favor the elites at the expense of the rest of the people.

After the fall, people eventually recovered and began to farm. But since land was considered a source of power and protection, land was not inherited equally. It was usually given to the oldest son. Eventually there would be a few people who were landlords with many living on the land who had nothing. This process would take generations. The landlord ruled the land he owned. His tenants were his subjects. He would be their judge, and leader in war. The landlord made war when they wanted and sometimes fought against their king. If the land were divided, it would put the estate in danger. Serfs belonged to the land. Everything was under control of the landlord. If the land was sold, the serfs went with the land. Often, landlords would fight with one another. The landlords would spend their time defending their territory, gaining new land, and spending their money on goods that would show their wealth. They rarely used their wealth to improve their lands. In this time, serfs were not capable of acquiring property. Whatever they acquired was acquired to their master and he could take it from them at any time. All cultivation and improvement would be carried on at the expense of the master. Some countries even had this as late as the 1700's. The serfs could not acquire anything beyond their daily maintenance. Since the serfs were not rewarded for extra work, why work any harder than necessary? Smith wrote, "The pride of man makes him love to domineer, and nothing mortifies him so much as to be obliged to condescend to persuade his inferiors." (Smith, page 299) The rich would prefer the services of slaves to freemen. The lords only knew how to protect their territories. They were not good investors.

Smith compares the laws of inheritance in Europe to the use of capitalism in the North American colonies. After the land was taken by the colonies, it was available to claim by the colonists. With plenty of timber, land, and resources, there was much profit to be had. Where there is incentive, there is much growth. Where there is no incentive, there is slow growth. The customs of Europe did not allow for small proprietors. Because of the laws of inheritance in Europe, land and property tended to consolidate. In the colonies, there was a multiplication of small proprietors. Smith wrote, "A small proprietor, however, who knows every part of his little territory, who views it with all the affection which property, especially small property, naturally inspires, and who upon that account takes pleasure not only in cultivating, but in adorning it, is generally of all improvers the most industrious, the most intelligent, and the most successful." (Smith, page 299)

Smith noted that men will work very hard when they are well paid. Men will work harder still if they have ownership in the business. No mention was made of men working hard for their 'work family', or for the sake of work ethic, or to better the company, or pizza parties or ping pong tables in the office. (Smith pages 69,70) Smith noted that the colonies prospered because they had plenty of good land, natural resources, and they could manage their own affairs. The wealth of the colonies came from each person being able to profit from their labor. (Smith pages 438,442)

According to Smith, a nation's economy and resources depend on the skill of the labor force. (Smith, page 4) He noted that if men were skilled and had incentive, the nation would have a strong and prosperous economy. Capitalism lends an 'invisible hand' to promote the virtues of society based on the cumulative efforts of each person to gain wealth. (Smith, page 349) The wealth of a nation doesn't come from taking wealth from another nation. As each person strives to be wealthy, their total combined effort makes the nation wealthy.

It stands to reason that the best way to maximize our effort is to have everyone be a skilled worker who has an ownership stake in his or her business. That is, everyone is their own entrepreneur. This may be the ultimate expression of true capitalism. Each person works to make their own fortune. But this is not what we have today.

True Capitalism seems to work the best with a free nation. Where there are lords, the rulers decide what the citizens or serfs can have. With communism and even socialism, the State decides the affairs of business. But with capitalism, property division is left to the action of the markets.

Labor is the original definition of value. Labor is the first cost for any good. How much labor can you command with the money that you have? (Smith, page 28) In a market, competitive prices determine the value of a good or service. What people are willing to pay determines its value. All goods, services, and labor are subject to the laws of supply and demand. No one individual can determine the balance of trade between nations. That is best done by a free market where prices are subject to supply and demand.

If supply is plentiful and a good is common, it is sold at a discount. If a good is scarce and supply is limited, the good commands a premium. This is in relation to demand. If the quantity demanded is low, the goods will be priced at a discount. If the quantity demanded is high, the goods will command a premium. Perhaps there may even be competitive bidding. Each factor functions in relation to the other. The generally agreed upon price is called the market price.

The competition between companies is likely to yield lower prices and higher quality that more closely matches what the customers want. This is to induce customers to buy from them rather than their competitors. The lower cost and higher quality will allow the consumer to get more value for their money, which will allow them to buy more goods & services. The idea is an ever-expanding standard of living. We can do and get more for less.

Adam Smith was an early advocate of the division of labor and mass production. He wrote about how the division of labor can drastically increase what a factory can produce. In essence, when a person has one part of a job, they can develop an expertise that allows them to be much more productive than a novice. There is a synergy in operating together that allows men to produce many times what could be produced by all the men if they worked separately. In Smith's example, he noted that a small factory could produce as many as 48,000 pins in a day. This would be much more than what a group of men could do separately. Economies favor manufacturing because it is much easier to gain an economy of scale. (Smith pages 8, 9) It is much easier for a system to do thousands of very simple tasks than it is to do a few complicated tasks. Switching tasks takes a lot more time than you might think. When you think about it, switching jobs or careers can take even more risk, time, and effort. This can be why switching jobs can often be so painful. This is especially true if you need more training. Who pays for the training and pays the bills?

Life before the Industrial Revolution was not easy. Most people worked their entire lives, usually in farming. The average workday could be ten to twelve hours per day. Education was some reading, writing, and basic math. If a person was lucky, they may be able to obtain a small farm or business. Others would work for someone else for their career. There was no retirement. That was an invention of the 20th century. If you couldn't work, you would either live with your grown children or go to a 'poor farm'. For many, becoming competent at their job and supporting one's family was considered success. (7) Most citizens of the United States were hopeful of a better future. (8) Life was hard in early America. But there was a hope of upward mobility. People had hope that if they worked hard, they might become wealthy.

People in Early America were not as heartless to the poor as you may believe. In 1964, conservative candidate Barry Goldwater wrote, "Let welfare be a private concern.

Let it be promoted by individuals and families, by churches, private hospitals, religious service organizations, community charities and other institutions that have been established for this purpose." This does not reflect the relief programs that were available in Early America. While able bodied men and women were put to work in exchange for provisions, children and those who were ill received care. The local governments would help the poor. The federal government was much smaller than it is today. It would only intervene if there was a crisis. Sometimes, young men could gain apprenticeships to start a career. Relief was minimal, but it provided for the needs of those who could not afford better. In early America, the solution to joblessness was for the community to provide jobs to able bodied men and women so that they could support themselves. (9)   In England, prospects for the poor were far different. The workhouses were run like prisons. Provisions for the poor were dirty, meager, and overcrowded.   Children had no hope of improving their life through education. There was also a belief that the poor had themselves to blame for their condition. (10)

Benefits of Capitalism

There have been benefits to capitalism. Capitalist countries have done better than communist nations. With free elections, there is a much lower threat of violence. Rule of law and civil rights usually ensure that we won't be prosecuted unfairly. We enjoy many freedoms that communist countries do not have. At our best, we have a higher standard of living than many other countries. We also have a higher standard of living and more purchasing power than in generations past. You only have to compare our life to those of our ancestors in colonial America. James Polk grew up in a small house with no plumbing, running water, or electricity. Diets were much simpler. There was no such thing as technology. Two hundred years ago, people did not have the tons of consumer choices that we have now. (11) Today, the middle class build homes that our forefathers could only dream of having. We have cars and can travel to any place in the world within a day. We have running water, plumbing, electricity, and foods from all around the world at our grocery stores. We have food pouring out of our farms and factories. The problem is that it does not always make it to the poorest. Instead, it goes to waste. In some instances, corporations would rather waste food than give it away to those who need it. (12)

Criticism of Capitalism

The United States seems to be heading towards a 'winner take all' or 'dog eat dog' approach. The 1% hoard their massive stockpiles of wealth while the homeless starve in the streets. No consideration seems to be given to the poor even if they are ill or children. (13, 14, 15, 16) Taxes on the wealthy have never been lower while our homeless problem continues. Those in the Forbes Top 400 list likely pay a lower tax rate than we do! (17) Even in early colonial America, the children and the ill were given shelter if they needed it. Those who were unemployed were given food and shelter in exchange for working. But these days, it's every man for himself. If you are starving in the street, you should just 'get a job'. It seems that inequality is growing every day. The rich get richer while the poor get poorer.

Much debate has been had on poverty, but we must do better!

Once corporations grow to sufficient size, they can take advantage of workers to pay them as little as possible. This drives down the workers standard of living and keeps people living in poverty. Adam Smith wrote, "A man must live by his work, and his wages must at least be sufficient to maintain him. They must even upon most occasions be some-what more; otherwise, it would be impossible for him to bring up a family, and the race of such workmen could not last beyond the first generation." (Smith, page 57) Yet today, the working poor must work hard then apply for public benefits. Those responsible should be ashamed! (18, 19, 20, 21) Even in 1776, Smith noted that employers have the advantage. When you think of the situation, it makes sense. Those hiring have all the information of job candidates and the money. It could be argued that since companies are fewer in number, they have favorable terms. Years ago, employers could combine much more easily, and workers were sometimes forbidden from banding together. In the early 1900s, laws were passed that made collective bargaining easier. I would add that due to the advantages of corporate size, they can afford to hire the best negotiator. We only have our individual selves to compete against a corporation that can use synergy and resources to its advantage. Remember, at a certain size, an organization can operate with extreme efficiency that a group of separate individuals can never hope to match. (Smith, page 56) Since the corporations have more money, they can hold out longer. They have far more reserves from their accumulated wealth. With the volume of their business, they can get far better terms than you or I could ever hope to have. Smith noted that in his time, employers collaborated to be sure to keep the wages artificially low and may work to squeeze the workers as much as possible. (Smith, page 57)

Capitalism does contribute to inequality. Those who do well accumulate capital. Those who do the poorest will lose everything. It's not bad to work hard if you are well rewarded. Nor is it bad to be rewarded richly if you work hard. It's almost impossible for everyone to be able to earn the same results. Let's say that you give two people an acre of land to farm. They will probably harvest a different amount of crops. Perhaps the richer farmer puts in more time. Or the richer farmer is lucky to get more rain or sunshine on their land. It is impossible to guarantee equal results. But you can provide equal opportunity by giving each person a share of land and equal access to seeds and tools. In a free society, you will have people who do better than others and become rich. The problem is when the rich use their advantage to oppress their workers. We need a societal safety net to pick up those who fall.

The growth of capitalism has increased many problems as it has increased economic activity. Trash and pollution continue to be a global problem. At the dawn of the 20th century, capitalism began to change our society from producers to consumers. Rather than repair an item, we just buy new. I have often found that it is now cheaper to buy a new item than repair it. I find that it is more difficult to find replacement parts. But this creates garbage that fills our landfills. One pitfall of capitalism is that it must always expand. Now, we replace perfectly useful items because they are no longer in fashion. We even must contend with 'planned obsolescence'. Goods are purposefully made to have a short life span so that we can buy more of them. Long gone are the appliances that last decades. We are convinced that we need more stuff. Because we buy more stuff, we must make more and work more. This puts us on a constant hamster wheel to acquire more stuff that we don't even need. If we did not buy as much some of us would not have to work as hard. John Stuart Mill proposed the steady-state economy. He proposed that if we consume just what we need, we could work at reduced hours and spend the extra time enjoying our families. (22)

Capitalism has caused the consumption of nearly the entire world. Our forests and natural lands are in danger of being consumed. The pollution and consumption are contributing to climate change. We must have some part of our land for nature to provide necessary things like oxygen and waste reduction. Our planet is like an aquarium. When I was six, I was allowed to have an aquarium. I stocked as many fish into the aquarium as I could fit. Within a few weeks, all the fish died. What we did not know was that the aquarium, like this planet, has a limited carrying capacity. You must reserve space for the water to replenish oxygen and eliminate the waste produced by the fish. We must also have unused natural space to replenish oxygen, absorb pollution, and protect biodiversity. Otherwise, we may choke to death on our own poisons and CO_2.

Corporations are even trying to influence how we eat, and they are making us sick. There are food scientists whose job it is to make food products with the optimized levels of salt, fat, and sugar so that we find them irresistible. Rather than having a light snack, we feel compelled to eat the whole package. This serves to fatten our waistlines and corporate bottom lines. Our level of obesity has skyrocketed. (23,24) We need to resist the temptations that corporations place before us and live more responsibly.

Capitalism has made us dumber. Corporations thrive on economies of scale and the division of labor. It stands to reason that it makes sense to have each task split to be as simple as possible. As we divide labor, we can maximize efficiency. The idea is that we become an expert at a tiny part of the manufacturing process. But these tasks tend to be very simple and repetitive. We are trained to be specialists in a very small part of the business process. We may be experts at what we do, but we have no idea how we fit into the overall process. We have no ability to produce a product from scratch. We have no idea how to survive in the wild. When I visited the James Polk homestead, I learned that James Polk's father was able to build his house with his own hands. People learned to be carpenters, farmers, survivalists and whatever else they needed to be. Today, if we get lost in the woods, we might die. Our forefathers lived in those woods their entire lives. But we have become tiny cogs that are dependent on society. Without the products that are supplied by the economy, we would die. A prolonged problem in the supply chain could cause anarchy and death in the streets.

Karl Marx noted that every five to seven years, there would be a cycle of recovery then recession. (25) In the beginning of a business cycle, all goods and services produced are rarer because businesses are less willing and able to produce them. The value of the goods is more because demand is higher than supply. The market price people are willing to pay exceeds its cost in natural price. There is an investment made to produce more goods to gain from the demand for products. At a certain point, the businesses over produce. Once the markets are saturated, demand goes down, but supply remains high. The market price of the goods is now lower than the natural price because demand is lower than supply. When the demand for the goods at the cost falls, businesses must contract and reduce staff or close. The sale of the goods is no longer profitable. And then begins a new cycle. These cycles are very erratic. If we graphed economic growth, it would like a jagged sawtooth blade. There have always been lots of sharp ups and downs. I made this observation myself when watching the news. When there is growth, things are great. People are getting raises and buying lots more stuff. But when there is a downturn, people lose their jobs. People lose their homes, go bankrupt, families split up and people suffer. Losing a job is one of the most stressful things that can happen. (26) It is during these downturns that people's lives fall off the rails. This is another reason that we need to have a strong social safety net.

Throughout history, capitalism has been the most successful approach to economics. Many of us have an unparalleled standard of living that previous generations could never imagine. But our system is not by any means perfect. In the Gettysburg Address, President Lincoln refers to our government as "of the people, by the people, and for the people." (27) But neither our government nor business seem to remember this. Each person gets their vote. They are free to vote to look after their own interest. But this system is not serving the people. The people are best represented by the middle class. Being middle class is part of the American Dream. We don't have to live in a mansion, but we would like to be able to comfortably support our families. This dream is in jeopardy. The middle class is shrinking. (28) Even though Americans are more educated and more productive, real wages and purchasing power have been stagnant for over 40 years. Most of the gains have gone to higher paid workers, so the gains have not been evenly distributed. For 40 years, most of us have been getting paid the same or less to do more and more work! (29, 30, 31, 32, 33, 34) Our government is not serving the people unless the people can live comfortably. It is not the job of the government to let the wealthy get super rich while everyday people lose their homes and livelihoods. We need an economy and a country where if we work hard, we can achieve, succeed, and be richly rewarded. We need to think about the kind of society we want to have. We need a strong social safety net for those who fail because any one of us can come on hard times. We have come a long way, but we the American people must watch that we don't lose our standard of living.

The History of Consumerism

Two hundred years ago, we produced only what we needed. Life was much simpler and much harder. We washed our clothes by hand. We had to make all meals from scratch. Our only entertainment was books. But there wasn't much time for leisure. Electricity hadn't been invented yet. Machines and factories were much smaller. Some goods were shipped from other places, but they would be expensive. Our food was grown on local farms or taken from the local woods. If we wanted a house, we might build it with our own hands. At James Polk's homestead, James Polk's father built their house by hand. Nails were scarce. When it came time to move, the Polks would burn down the house so that it would be easier to recover the nails. But since then, we have gone from being producers to consumers. (11)

The factories and mass production allowed companies to make many goods cheaply. Previously, goods were made only if they were needed. But with mass production, producers would anticipate the demand for their product and push the many goods out to the consumers. This allowed products to be sold for much lower prices. This also provided an incentive for companies to push their many goods on to the customer. And so began our consumer culture. The companies felt a lot of pressure to sell all the goods they have made. If the companies overestimated their markets, they would pay the cost for the goods they didn't sell. If the companies find they have overproduced, they stop producing. If enough companies overproduce, this may cause a recession. You could argue that when they increased production, that would be a recovery. They would hire more people to produce. This mismatch between production and consumption is likely the cause for our economic cycles of recession and recovery.

The pressure to sell the goods produced gave birth to advertising. Let's convince the customers that they need this new item. Why keep the old when you can have the new? It is much more efficient for a factory to make goods than for people to make the goods at home. Every good that can be made more efficiently represents an opportunity for companies to make money. Over time, we shifted from being a nation that produced what we needed to becoming a nation that consumed what others produced. Each improvement on a product was an opportunity to sell yet another product. This produced an incentive for companies to convince consumers to buy goods because they were new. Don't repair what you need, buy new. Is something out of style? Buy something newer. Not only did companies try to convince consumers to buy what the company had produced, the companies would even try to change the public's opinion to sell more products. Lucky Strikes successfully convinced the public that smoking was not 'unladylike'. They went from selling 14 billion cigarettes to

40 billion cigarettes in a year.   We have companies influencing our morals and beliefs so that they can sell more products. (35)

Decades ago, companies prided themselves on making products that would last. Appliances would last for decades. But it became more profitable to convince customers to constantly replace their possessions. Let's buy new goods with the latest styles and new functions. Then we just throw out our old items. It isn't much of a logical step to get to planned obsolescence. (36) Companies now just assume that consumers will replace their items at certain intervals. Why should they make goods last? Why not set expectations low? You aren't buying an item to own forever. You are buying a device that is set to last three years. Even if you take care of your device, the company will just stop supporting it after a set amount of time. If you want their device in your life, you must commit to buying new every few years. If there is a problem with the device, you are required to have the company repair it. At this point in history, it is just cheaper and easier to buy a new device. This is another example of how the companies have power because they are larger than the individual. If you want to have a certain product, you must play by the rules of the different companies. Businesses don't have to worry about quality anymore. They have convinced us to constantly keep the latest style and functions. Why worry about quality if we are going to buy new soon anyways? This has caused the level of pollution and garbage to skyrocket. We now stuff landfills with perfectly usable goods that we didn't need to replace. We burn gas and cause pollution for these goods. We use up our resources to make items that could have been used longer. We are on this constant hamster wheel for more and bigger stuff.

In some business models, we don't even own the products we buy. The latest scam involves subscription services. Let's say that you buy a car with heated seats or remote start. Not only do you have to pay for the item to be installed in your car, but you also must pay a monthly or yearly subscription service fee to keep that item activated. (37) Talk about a money grab. You pay for it once, then you pay for it for the rest of the life of your vehicle. Why don't they just sell you the part for a set price? Why do they make you pay them forever? If you don't pay, they deactivate the function. This just shows that Big Business is playing games. I understand that companies need to make a profit. So why don't they sell the option for a profitable price? If you don't use the item, it doesn't reduce the cost they paid to produce it. They don't spend any more money if you use the part. But they lose a potential source of income. Why don't they just price the part fairly? If I were presented options for these subscription services, I would just walk out of the dealership and keep my old car. A recent survey suggests that most people would agree with me. (37) Maybe there should be a law. There was a policy change put in place for medical devices for sleep apnea. It was a game changer. Previously, companies would 'rent' patients their medical devices such as CPAP machines. Companies could give a patient a machine that they may use for five, ten, or more years. The company would buy the machine, then charge rent to the patient for the rest of their life. The company would reap many times more than what the machine cost. But Medicare limited companies from renting medical devices for more than 13 months. After the initial rental period, the patient owns the machines. Now, patients and insurance companies spend less money for the devices. The medical companies are now more motivated to help the patients keep their machines updated. This is where the law protects consumers. Patients pay less and are more likely to have updated machines. Insurance companies pay less, so we premium holders should also pay less. The only losers are the medical device companies that can't charge a fortune for old machines. (38) Medicare tends to lead the trends for the medical reimbursement industry. So, all the other insurance providers soon followed Medicare's policy. This is an example of the federal government leading by example.

Big Business has drastically altered how we live our lives. Don't try to tell me that individuals and companies are on an even level. Big Business is much more efficient at making items and negotiating terms in their favor due to their size. That's why we need to have someone protect us from corporations.

Consumerism encouraged the nightmare customer. You know the ones. The Karens and the Chads. Those who throw a fit and always demand to see the manager. It turns out that the department stores set up the conditions to create these monster customers. Nobody wants to be at the bottom of the social ladder. Most people can't afford servants. But it just feels so good to have people wait on you. The stores came up with the idea that their employees should adopt servile mannerisms so that the average person could feel like they were wealthy when they shopped. (39) Perhaps it made the customer feel that they were better than the store employees. Department store owners Harry Gordon Selfridge, John Wanamaker, and Marshall Field are credited with promoting the slogan 'The customer is always right.' (40) The customer is not ALWAYS right. Sometimes customers are unreasonable. It's a balancing act. Companies should try to make customers happy if the requests are reasonable. But if a customer is more trouble than they are worth, the employee should have the freedom to cut the customer loose. But companies just don't seem to care. Many times, the companies expect employees to put up with intolerable abuse so that the owners can make a few more bucks.

Consumer Safety

Before Theodore Roosevelt passed the Pure Food and Drug Act in 1906, companies could put anything in food with no information given to the consumer. (41) The Pure Food and Drug Act forced companies to reveal what they put in foods and limited ingredients used. But no thought of safety was given to products until Ralph Nader began his lifelong consumer safety campaign. Before certain laws were passed, companies had no responsibility for the safety of their products. (42)

In 1965, Ralph Nader published Unsafe at Any Speed. The book proposed that many American automobiles were unsafe to operate. Due to Nader's efforts, Congress enacted the National Traffic and Motor Vehicle Safety Act. (43) Much progress has been made in auto safety since the 1970s. Without Nader's influence, the auto industry would never have adopted safety standards on their own. You could argue that millions owe Nader their lives due to the lifesaving safety measures installed in motor vehicles.

In 1968, seven volunteer law students, (Nader's Raiders) evaluated the operation of the FTC (Federal Trade Commission). This led Richard Nixon to upgrade the activity of the FTC for consumer protection in the 1970s. (44) Nader founded the group Public Citizen to lobby for consumer rights. (45) Nader's work was credited for the enactment of the Freedom of Information Act, Foreign

Corrupt Practices Act, Clean Water Act, Consumer Product Safety Act, and the Whistleblower Protection Act. (46, 47, 48, 49) The Consumer Product Safety Act established the Consumer Product Safety Commission that was tasked with ensuring that products sold to consumers met certain safety standards. The law requires all products to be safety tested before they are sold.

Activism and government intervention is a necessary part of our society. We need protection from companies who would sell us cheaply made unsafe goods. This is another example where government oversight improved our standard of living.

——

THE INDUSTRIAL REVOLUTION & PROGRESS

THE INDUSTRIAL REVOLUTION AND PROGRESS

Before the Industrial Revolution, most businesses were based in agriculture. The cities were centers for banking and commerce with a few small factories. Many jobs were in farms, shops, or small factories. Most non-farming jobs were in the city. People worked ten-to-twelve-hour days. They considered themselves successful if they could become competent at a job and support their family. Americans worked hard but they felt optimistic about the opportunity for a better future.

With the Industrial Revolution came the machines, big factories, and mass production. For America, this process started in the mid 1800's and lasted until the early 1900's. It started in England in the 1700's. There were several reasons that the Industrial Revolution was so successful in America. We had plenty of untapped resources such as timber, coal, and metals. Europe could not hope to match us in resources. When railroads began to form, we had an increased need for steel. Since the railroads sped up the transportation of goods, there were new markets for new goods. Once word was spread about the opportunities in America, plenty of young immigrants came. The factories had their pick of young, hardworking men. Soon, this would cause an overage of eager, hardworking laborers. The

American government took a hands-off approach to the economy. The business owners could do whatever they wanted. Plenty of new inventions made for new goods and new methods of production. Over decades, the U.S. was able to make great investments in transportation using waterways and railroads. This allowed goods to be quickly shipped across the country and opened new markets. (1)

Since so many new inventions were applied to farming, the nation could shift its focus to manufacturing. During the Industrial Revolution, people moved from the country to the cities. At the beginning of this process, six percent of the population lived in cities. In the end, nearly everyone lived in cities. Before industrialization, many goods were made by skilled craftsmen who were able to make a decent living. But the factories only needed unskilled labor that was cheaper. The factories put many artisans out of business. Often, factories would hire women and children because they could be paid half the wages of the men. Even pregnant women and children were expected to work 16-hour days. Before, families worked together on their farms. In factories, many men had to leave their families behind to find work in the city. Even if the family lived in the city, the grueling work hours left scarcely any time for family. People worked, slept, and repeated the cycle until they died. (2) The factory workers often lived in unsafe and disease-ridden urban slums. (3)

Working in the factories was grueling, dangerous, and oppressive. The lighting and ventilation were poor. Smoke was often a problem that caused many eye and lung issues. The machines and workstations had no safety protocols. Accidents happened frequently. Children as young as five were hired to operate machinery. Owners had no legal or financial reason to care about the safety of their workers.

With massive immigration to the U.S., wages were cheap because there were so many workers. Workers were easily replaced and had no bargaining power. If a worker died, the owner had their pick from a crowd of other workers struggling to find a job. If a worker was injured or disabled, they would just be fired. Many worked 12-to-16-hour days 6 days a week. Workers were lucky to have one-hour breaks for lunch. The factories liked to hire children because they were easy to bully. Small children were often abused. If a child fell asleep at work, they would be beaten. The work pace at the factories was fast paced and brutal. In the past, families worked together in the fields and could converse and spend time with each other. There was time at the end of the day to socialize. But in the factory, talking was kept to a minimum to increase production. There was scarcely any time left to spend with family. For a time, the Combination Acts forbid unions. (4)

Not only did corporations grow to oppress their workers, but they also cheated their customers. Adam Smith stated that competition would cause companies to offer lower prices for better quality goods. But by the end of the 19th century, corporations would find ways to limit competition to maximize their profits. Some corporations grew to dominate their markets by growing and buying the competition until they were the only supplier of their product. Other companies were able to make deals so that they could work together to eliminate the competitive nature of the market. The mega corporations would use different tactics to keep new companies from being able to enter the market. These 'robber barons' could decide the fates of other companies by using price discrimination and forbidding vendors and customers from doing business with certain companies. The larger corporations might purchase stocks in competing firms or sit on the boards of competing companies. Once the corporations eliminated the limits set by competition, they could raise prices, lower wages, and cut corners to lower quality. There would be no incentives for the companies to innovate to make better products. The customers and employees would be the ones to lose because they had no other options. People had to just take it or leave it. (5, 6, 7)

Something had to give. The robber barons had become the new feudal lords. Capitalism was supposed to use competition to give the people better products for lower prices. But something went wrong. With the power of division of labor, mass production, and unethical business practices, some firms were able to grow to gigantic sizes to eat their competitors until they were the only companies left. The policy of laissez faire had become economic anarchy! But with anarchy comes oppression.

When Jean-Jacques Rousseau wrote The Social Contract, he argued that in order to have freedom, you had to live in a society that would ensure your right to freedom. You can't have absolute freedom if it includes the freedom to constrain the freedom of others. You must limit the freedoms of some in order to ensure that others have freedom. Otherwise, the strong will oppress those who are weaker. Large nations will take over small nations. Large corporations will run small companies out of business if they are left to their own devices. (8, 9) After the fall of the Roman Empire in the West, Europe fell into chaos. The people fled to the countryside for their safety. Survival was difficult because everyone had become dependent on the Roman Empire to provide for their needs. Society had fallen into disarray and there was no government in charge. But no society lives by anarchy for long. Within a few hundred years, the small villages and farms had become estates ruled by feudal lords who had sworn loyalty to a king. These feudal lords owned the land and the people on the land. (10, 11) Larger organizations will always out compete smaller organizations. With enough time and people, disorganized groups will merge into large organizations. So large nations and mega-corporations may be inevitable. In America, the people had taken enough price gouging, inferior goods, and slave wages. It was time to take action!

The Progressive Movement

Throughout the history of America, there were those who would demand that we improve our society so that it would work for all Americans. By the end of the 19th century, the Progressive movement had begun to have some traction. The people had enough of the poverty and exploitation caused by unrestrained capitalism, immigration, and political corruption. The first step was the Sherman Antitrust Act passed in 1890. This law forbade the practice of having several competing companies transfer their shares to a joint board of trustees to manage the companies together into a pool. This was the first attempt to curb the monopolies that were dominating corporate America. It was a sign of the beginning of a movement. But some of the terms were vague and hard to define. The law wasn't used effectively until the early 1900's when Theodore Roosevelt was elected president. (12) Even though President Taft bust more trusts, Theodore Roosevelt was known as the 'trustbuster' because he was the first president to effectively use the Anti-Trust legislation. He busted 44 trusts including the Standard Oil Company and the Northern Securities Company that owned the biggest railroad company. (13)

President Roosevelt was considered a leader of the progressive movement. He championed his "Square Deal" domestic policies, promising the average citizen fairness, breaking of trusts, regulation of railroads, and pure food and drugs. He also created the U.S. Department of Commerce and Labor. Roosevelt felt that the government should control the relations between corporations and labor so that each side would have justice. (14) In 1906, Roosevelt passed the Meat Inspection Act and the Pure Food and Drug Act. These acts banned misleading labels and the inclusion of harmful chemicals in food and drugs. The bills passed with help from Upton Sinclair's The Jungle. It was a book that detailed the exploitation and unsanitary conditions at the Chicago Meat Packing Company. (15) In 1914, the Clayton Antitrust Act was passed. This was a stronger anti-trust law that prohibited anti-competitive mergers & predatory pricing. This act also allowed individuals to sue corporations and upheld the rights to form unions and protest. The Federal Trade Commission was formed to enforce this law. (16) This didn't solve all the problems with capitalism, but it was a good start. It set the precedent that the government should get involved to restrain big business so that workers and customers aren't exploited. For a time, it ended 'laissez faire' capitalism. Unfortunately, more progress would have to wait. Once World War I started, the Progressive movement lost steam.

The Roaring Twenties, the Great Depression, and the New Deal

After World War I and the Spanish Flu Epidemic ended, there was the Roaring Twenties. For a time, things were going great. The U.S. was recovering from World War I and there was demand for consumer goods due to the invention of the automobile and electricity. The U.S. was able to use its war time building capacity to produce goods for new markets across the world. (17) Another influencing factor was the new immigration control laws that came about in the 1920s. The first immigration law passed in 1917 required immigrants over 16 to pass a literacy test. But this was not enough for everyone. In 1924, the U.S. passed the Johnson-Reed Act that implemented quotas on how many new immigrants could come into the U.S to approximately 350,000. (18) While this legislation was discriminatory, it did work to solve the issue of too many workers looking for jobs. This approach likely lifted wages by limiting the supply of workers. But the exclusionary philosophy may have come with a price. At the end of the Twenties came the Great Depression. Several factors are blamed for causing the Great Depression including the stock market crash of 1929, the effects of the Smoot-Hawley Tariff, bank failures, and the collapse of the money supply. (19)

When Franklin Delano Roosevelt became president in March 1933, he began his program called the New Deal. This program would cause lasting changes to our society that are still affecting us even today. President Roosevelt's first task was to tackle the issues the U.S. had with banking and the Stock Market. In 1933, he passed the Emergency Banking Act, the 1933 Banking Act, and the Securities Act of 1933. Roosevelt's first act would be passing the Emergency Banking Act. First, there was a bank holiday. This would allow the government to inspect the banks to make sure they were fit to reopen. The bank closures also stopped the panicked withdrawals that threatened to bankrupt the financial system. Once the banks reopened, the Federal Reserve Banks issued assets to cover the demands for withdrawals from the customers. Within two weeks, the customers had returned half of the currency that they had withdrawn during the panic. Once the bank panic subsided, America could focus on the long road to recovery and Roosevelt could focus on the long-term issues with banking and securities. (20, 21, 22) Another important piece of legislation was the Banking Act of 1933, also called the Glass-Steagall Act. This act separated commercial banks from investment banks. Commercial banks who held individual's money were no longer allowed to invest substantially in securities. They could only have 10 percent of total income from securities. Investment banks were no longer allowed to have close connections with commercial banks. This is important because the stock market crash of 1929 caused many banks to fail. Since the money in the banks were tied to stock market securities, the crash caused the banks to lose much of the money that the customers had deposited. Once word spread that the banks were losing money, there was a panic for customers to take out their money before it was all gone. This Act also gave tighter regulation powers to the Federal Reserve System. Finally, the FDIC (Federal Deposit Insurance Corporation) was formed to insure every account for $2,500. This was a lot of money in the 1930's. Currently, the FDIC insures every account for $250,000. This was important because the economy needed for the consumers to have confidence that the banks would not lose their money. (23) The final piece of the first part of the New Deal was the Securities Act of 1933. This Act required companies to provide financial information about their companies to back up the claims that they made. It was now specifically illegal to make fraudulent claims about a company to sell stocks or bonds. The power to regulate stocks was taken away from the states and given to the federal government. In 1934, the Securities and Exchange Commission was established to regulate the securities markets. Before these laws, companies could make wild claims about the profitability of their stocks while releasing none of the facts about their financials. Companies could put anything they wanted into food and make any claims about medicines. There were no standards and no information had to be given. Any claims could be made with no one to check that the claims were true. This is an example where the government had to step in for the greater good of society. (24)

The Second New Deal was enacted between 1935 and 1936. This program made for even greater reforms to our way of life. The National Labor Relations Act of 1935 guaranteed the right for workers to organize trade unions, practice collective bargaining, and strike. This act was intended to balance the bargaining power between unions and employers. The National Labor Relations Board was made to enforce workers' right to organize. (25) This is an example where the Federal Government supported Union activity and is a departure from previous approaches shown by the Combinations Act that had forbidden workers to combine to unionize. (26) This was the start of the rise of the unions.

The Works Progress Administration of 1935 employed millions of jobseekers for work on the nation's infrastructure. These projects built many parks, schools, and roads. (27) This is an example of the government directly providing jobs that are needed. This was a drastic departure from the laissez-faire non-involvement of the past. There are some functions that can't be accomplished by the market and must be provided by the government for the public good. Sometimes the government must purchase goods and enact projects to ensure that the public has what it needs.

The Social Security Act of 1935 was the last major act passed in that year. This law created unemployment insurance and the Social Security program that we all use. At that time, the United States was the only modern society without any social security system. People in poverty were drastically reduced because there was now income for those too old to work. This program was funded by payroll taxes. We pay into this system when we work. When we retire, we begin receiving income from Social Security. This program provided the first real opportunity for retirement. Mass retirement was an invention of the Twentieth Century. Few people had access to a pension, so most people worked until they died or spent their old age in squalor. (28, 29) But now we are in danger of losing our retirement and returning to poverty in our old age.

In 1938, the Fair Labor Standards Act was passed. This is a landmark event that made our way of life possible. This law created a minimum wage. The law also established time and a half pay for overtime worked over 40 hours in a week. Oppressive child labor was outlawed. (30, 31) This law put into place practices that have been demanded by workers for decades. This is an example of the government working to protect the people. Children belong in school and not in oppressive sweatshops. When the children were taken out of the labor pool, the price of labor for the remaining workers could only increase. The minimum wage was put in place to ensure that workers could support their families and rise out of poverty. For decades, workers demanded 8 hours for work, 8 hours for leisure, and 8 hours for sleep. (32) The overtime provision set the expectation of an 8-hour workday by providing extra pay for when employees work 'overtime'.

Forty hours of regular time divided by eight hours makes for five workdays. This policy set the tone for the modern two-day weekend as we know it. Before these provisions, people worked up to 16-hour days, 6 days a week, for whatever the owners could get away with paying. Workers would go home to filthy, crowded apartments because that was all they could afford.

THE UNIONS

The union movement had a rough start from the very beginning. According to old English common law, it was illegal for workers to 'combine' to bargain for better wages. In the 19th century, there were even several cases in America where union organizers were convicted. The penalties weren't severe, but the precedent was set for a time. On occasion, there would be violence at the picket lines. Fights would sometimes start between strikers and the replacement workers known as 'scabs'. There were also violent conflicts between the union members and the police. The unions would often have to fight the corporations and the government for their right to exist. It wasn't until the case of Commonwealth v. Hunt in 1842 that the legality of unions was established. (33, 34) The Clayton Antitrust Act of 1914 gave employees the right to strike. But Unions prospered even more once the Labor Relations Act passed in 1935. This act established the union as a legitimate institution. (35, 36)

With the poor working conditions and pay brought about by the Industrial Revolution and unregulated capitalism, it was only natural that workers would want to join together to counteract the unfair advantages that employers held. These labor unions came about because many workers had little political support due to being immigrants and women who were not allowed to vote. Before the New Deal in the 1930s, laborers had been demanding change for decades. The unions served an important role as an early lobbyist for workers' rights. The labor movement had championed collective bargaining, the 8-hour workday, and safety standards.

Unions serve important functions in our society. Collective bargaining helps to counteract the advantage that employers hold over workers. Since employers have the information about all job candidates, their greater knowledge gives them an advantage. Employers have more money and can use their size to hire experts in fields such as negotiations. The average worker is not an expert negotiator. If workers don't bargain together, they are likely to be undercut by the lowest and most desperate bidder. But collective bargaining helps to level the playing field for workers. All workers get a fairer share because they are working together. Unions also bargain for improved safety protections, increased job security, and even generous pension benefits. Other benefits can include a sense of community, improved workplace equality, and protection from unfair dismissal. The unions serve as a standard bearer for what non-union workplaces should provide.

Think of it this way. Let's say that job candidates are like card players at the casino. Each of the players are competing to 'win' the job. Each player knows only the information from the hand they have. The company or hiring manager would be the dealer. In this case, the dealer knows their hand and the hands of every other player. The dealer knows all. Don't you think the dealer would have an incredible advantage in this game? Who do you think would win?

There are a few drawbacks to unions. Workers must pay union dues. One would expect that the wages gained by a better bargain would cover any dues taken. Union shops do have higher employee expenses than non-union shops. There should also be oversight to ensure that there is no corruption in the union. Another issue with a union involves the incentive to work hard. A hard-working employee will not receive any more pay than an employee who is hardly working. It is difficult to reward high achieving employees or dismiss poorly performing employees. Union shops also provide less flexibility. When bargaining, unions need to make sure that workers get their fair share. But they must also be careful that their employer can still afford to operate. Otherwise, everyone will be out of a job once the business closes. (38) The best union relations involve a partnership where the unions and the management can work together to ensure workers' rights and corporate profitability.

How did labor reform turn out for us?

Even after President Roosevelt passed the New Deal, America's struggles weren't yet over. America had to struggle through the Great Depression, making reforms, and World War II. During the war, there were many sacrifices. There were high taxes, supply shortages, and rationing. But the decades after the war are generally remembered as being a time of great prosperity. The three decades after World War II are often called the Golden Age of Capitalism. The middle class as we know it was created during this time. Fair wages allowed many to buy homes, stock their homes with new appliances, and drive their new cars to take vacations. Unemployment during this time averaged less than 5 percent. In the 1950s, the economy grew 37% and the average family had 30% more purchasing power than at the beginning. Inflation was kept in check. President Eisenhower built the Interstate Highway System. The prosperity was brought about by a new consumerism. Credit Card debt was also a new invention. Society was hooked on buy now, pay later. (38,39) Between the projects built in the 1950's and the projects from Roosevelt's New Deal, we built much of the infrastructure that we still use today. These would be roads, bridges, buildings, and institutions that were built on a scale that has not been reached since. Nostalgia for the 1950's comes to mind for many. It was a time of prosperity and innocence for most. This prosperity carried over into the 1960s. It wasn't until the 1970's that the United States suffered from the twin woes of economic stagnation and inflation. (40) Our prosperity at this time was due to several factors. Post War demand boosted the consumer economy. Government projects and government jobs financed by higher taxes also helped to create prosperity. The United States had the international advantage because most of its infrastructure was not damaged during the war. Strong unions and beneficial labor laws ensured the workers would be treated fairly.

How are we doing now?

The Gross Domestic Product & Dow Jones were both at historical highs before the pandemic. Worker output per hour has never been higher. (41, 42, 43) The politicians in charge may point to these statistics to show you the good job they are doing. They say that we have nothing to worry about because the GDP and the Dow Jones are so high. But the average person isn't sharing in that prosperity. The

GDP does not tell you whether the results are shared amongst the people. The Dow Jones could rise to one million dollars, but that does you no good if you don't have a dollar to invest in it. While productivity is to the moon, wage increases are far behind. The rate of growth for productivity and wages has been growing bigger since 1979. According to data from the Economic Policy Institute, productivity has increased by 243% from 1979 to 2013 while wages have only increased by 108% for the same time period. During the postwar period of 1947 to 1979, there was strong shared wage growth. Of course, this only affects the 99%. While the top 1% saw wage increases of 138% from 1979 to 2013, the bottom 90% only received a wage increase of 15%. Another chart suggests that low wage workers saw a 5% DECREASE from 1979 to 2013. These numbers would be adjusted for inflation. (44, 45) It is true that wages increased, and that unemployment has generally been under 10 percent, but that's not the whole picture. (46) Every other metric has increased, and full employment no longer means you can pay your bills. Adjusted for inflation, median household income rose from $56,000/year in 1986 to approximately $75,000/year in 2022. Median household income has grown 33 percent over 37 years. (47) Since these numbers represent purchasing power, this may sound good. But there are several other factors that have caused purchasing power to increase. We are now more educated than ever. In 1986, 16 percent of workers had a college degree. Now, over 37 percent have a college degree. (48) So, it stands to reason that our wages would grow. Many may remember that in the 1950s the men would go to work, and the women would stay home and be housewives. At least that is what the magazines of the time would tell you. That may not be completely true. In 1967, 45 percent of married couple families had both husband and wife working. In 2011, approximately 55 percent of married couples had both adults working. Before the Great Recession, 60 percent of married households had both adults working. (49) When you account for more educated people working in a household, then it would be expected that purchasing power would rise. You would think that real purchasing power would increase by more than a paltry 33 percent over 37 years. The data suggests that real purchasing power for recent college graduates has fallen since the year 2000. (44) Yet prices for a college education and housing have been skyrocketing. Average annual college costs in real dollars have quadrupled since 1969. (50) In 1965, the average house cost approximately $25,000. Currently, the average house costs $450,000. (51) In 2021, 24 percent of homes sold were purchased by investors seeking to raise the prices in the home market. (52)

Top tax rates are at near historic lows. (53) Our public debt now stands at over $33 trillion. (54) Our GDP has never been higher, yet our infrastructure is in desperate need of repair. When graded, most of our infrastructure receives a grade of C- or less. (55, 56)

What happened to our country? How did we go from the nostalgic Golden Age of Capitalism to barely surviving? It's like the 1% have come and taken all our money overnight. The wealth of the 1% has skyrocketed while we have made no progress on the poverty rate since the 1970s. (57) This was no accident. Our plight is the result of greed and political complicity. Policies have been enacted to stack the deck in favor of the rich. In the next few chapters, we will explore just what happened over the last 50 years.

CHAPTER FIVE

———

NEOLIBERALISM AND HOW WE GOT TO THIS POINT

NEOLIBERALISM AND HOW WE GOT TO THIS POINT

In the 1970s, the economy fell victim to 'stagflation'. Growth was stagnant but there was still inflation. Companies were shutting down and laying off workers. Previously, high growth would lead to high inflation. Low growth would lead to high unemployment. This was the first time the U.S. economy saw high unemployment and high inflation at the same time. The problems in the economy were caused by large federal budget deficits caused by the Vietnam War and the war on poverty, the collapse of the Bretton Woods Agreement, and a sharp increase in the price of oil. This economic crisis caused a drastic shift in the U.S. economy and the national monetary policy. (1)

Wars are often expensive. Historically, wars cause a boost to the economy. But once the war was over, the boost was over. Since the Vietnam War required so much new machinery, the military expenditures caused rising inflation. The Vietnam War was the longest war in U.S. history. The government also boosted spending on social programs. President Johnson increased government spending, but there was not a sufficient increase in tax revenue. So, the National Debt soared. (2)

Lyndon B. Johnson was sworn in as President on November 22, 1963, after John F. Kenney was assassinated. One of his chief goals was the building of a 'Great Society'. This set of programs was also called the 'War on Poverty'.

These programs included job training programs, national work study programs, and loans to employers who offered jobs to the unemployed. During his presidency, Johnson was able to enact Medicare and Medicaid. These programs provided medical insurance for the elderly and the poor. Johnson was also able to pass education reform and the Housing and Urban Development Act of 1965. The Housing Act was in response to the mass exodus to suburbia that left the inner cities abandoned. In 1959, the poverty rate was approximately 24 percent. But by 1970, the poverty rate was cut to just over 12 percent. The nation has not made much progress in reducing poverty since 1970. (3,4) While these acts were the first step in reducing poverty in the U.S., not everyone was happy with Johnson's agenda. When Nixon began his presidency in 1968, he attempted to repeal or cut back many of the programs that Johnson enacted. Both the Great Society and the Vietnam War proved to be expensive. These programs served to increase inflation. But these programs weren't the only causes for the economic troubles in the 1970s.

After World War II, a foreign exchange system called the Bretton Woods Agreement was formed. Under this plan, the U.S. dollar was pegged to the value of gold and the currency of the 43 remaining member countries would be tied to the dollar. This system was intended to stabilize the international economy and spread prosperity around the world. The economy and the system worked well until the 1970s. The excessive spending from the Vietnam War and the Great Society caused a trade deficit that the U.S. was not able to maintain because they did not have enough gold. In 1972, Nixon suspended the Gold Standard, and the U.S. dollar could no longer be traded for gold. Before long, the international currencies were put on a floating system. The

U.S. dollar became a 'fiat' currency. This meant that the currency was backed by the government rather than gold or silver. The value of the U.S. dollar plummeted. The collapse of the Bretton Woods system is one of the factors that led to the out-of-control inflation. (5,6,7)

The price of oil was the final factor that challenged the U.S. economy in the 1970s. In 1973, Arab members of OPEC placed an embargo on the U.S. because we supported Israel during the Arab Israeli War. The price of oil quadrupled during this period. (8) In 1979, there was another oil shock that caused prices to more than double because of the Iranian Revolution. During this revolution, Iranian oil production sharply declined. This caused the high inflation to continue. (9) When you think about it, the price of oil is extremely important to our economy. We use gasoline to power our cars. Every item we make is transported hundreds or even thousands of miles using vehicles that burn gas. Oil is even used to make plastics. Many of our goods are made of plastic or contained in plastic. Oil is everywhere in our economy. Any increase in the price of oil will automatically cause an increase in the price of everything else.

The economy was a mess. By 1980, the Dow Jones (adjusted for inflation) had dropped to a level not seen since the 1950s. (10) The unemployment rate approached 10 percent in the late 1970s and topped 10 percent in the early 1980s. (11) Even the rate of poverty climbed in the late 1970s. (12) By the early 1980s, Paul Volcker had raised the Federal Reserve Rate to 20 percent! (13) The U.S. Fiscal Policy is to raise interest rates when inflation is high and lower interest rates if the economy needs a boost. The Federal Reserve Rate had never reached this height before, and it has not been that high since the 1980s. Median

Household Income adjusted for inflation was almost flat for the entire decade of the 70s. (14) Inflation for 1980 was over 13 percent. (15) Something had to be done. It was this crisis that led to a shift in our thinking about the economy. People wanted change. But did we make the right choices?

Neoliberalism and Supply Side Economics

In the 1980s, a new approach was taken by President Reagan. This philosophy goes by different names: Reaganomics, neoliberalism, and Free Market Capitalism. Reagan's policies included widespread tax cuts (especially to the wealthy), decreased social spending, increased military spending, increased budget deficits, massive deregulation, and increased interest rates to combat inflation. Free trade and globalization are also goals of neoliberalism. At the time, his policies resulted in more growth for the Dow Jones Industrial Average and the addition of 40 million jobs. Reagan cut the highest tax rate from 70% to 50%. The rate of inflation eased and drastically reduced unemployment. However, his policies started this country down the road to neoliberalism that created our wide inequality in wages. Critics argue that the deregulations Reagan implemented played a part in the Savings and Loan crisis and even the financial collapse of 2008. Nobel laureate Paul Krugman noted that the rich got richer, but "middle class incomes were barely higher than they had been a decade before and the poverty rate had risen." (16,17) Neoliberalism is sometimes called 'trickle-down' economics because we are told that the tax cuts to the wealthy will cause wealth to trickle down to the workers. The rich are supposed to take their extra money and invest it so that there will be more jobs. This assumes the rich will share their money.

Neoliberalism is similar to the laissez-faire policies that dominated our economy at the turn of the 20th century. The plan was to transfer as much control of the economy as possible to the market. This approach is most associated with Ronald Reagan and Margaret Thatcher. (18) A key component to consider is supply-side economics. This theory suggests that the best way to improve economic growth is to increase the supply of goods and services by cutting taxes on business and the wealthy. This approach contrasts the previous Keynesian theory that favored demand side economics. Supply side economists would argue that supply creates its own demand. If you give the rich enough money to build it, the customers will come. Government spending should also decrease because you are allowing the market to determine the direction of the economy. (19)

John Maynard Keynes developed his economic theories during the Great Depression. Keynesian theory dominated U.S. policy from the 1930s through to the 1980s. He stated that the government can generate demand for goods and services if needed. We call this demand-side economics. The government should increase spending in order to keep up the demand that would support economic growth. Under this system, aggregate demand was key. Aggregate demand consists of retail consumption, industrial investments, government spending, and exports. Government spending is a key component of the economy under Keynesian policy. Under neoliberalism, the government is assumed to be as small as possible. This is part of why our infrastructure suffers. A recent example of demand-side policy involves Obama's fiscal policy. He lowered interest rates, cut taxes for the middle class, and instituted a $787 billion stimulus package. (20)

With supply-side economics, the government focuses on letting businesses and the wealthy keep as much of their money as possible. The assumption is that the businesses will reinvest their extra money and create more jobs in America. There is nothing to guarantee that the money will be invested and that those investments will stay in the country. The rich could either save the money or send it overseas to create jobs in other countries. If a rich person receives extra money, they are most likely to invest it. With demand-side economics, the money tends to go to working class people. This involves tax cuts to the workers, tax credits, stimulus payments, increasing government spending, and government jobs. If a working-class person receives extra money, they are likely to spend it in the local economy. They may buy shoes for their kids, a new car, or even a new home. Their purchases will help local stores and businesses. It is more likely that money going to the working-class will benefit the U.S economy.

There are several issues with neoliberalism. Privatization may lead to using a free market approach to providing public services and goods. The goal in providing infrastructure, defense, education, and healthcare is not profit. The government's role is to provide a societal safety net because that is something that we collectively value. It has nothing to do with profit. Privatization can lead to these services being underfunded and ineffective. As we have seen at the turn of the 20th century, deregulation can also lead to monopolies. One congressional report lists Google, Amazon, Apple, and Facebook as being monopolies. (21) The free-market economy has also led to more economic instability. An International Money Fund report states that the increase in capital flows has increased the risk of downturns in the economy. Critics of neoliberalism have noted an increase in inequality and a decrease in social mobility. Some even state that globalization deprives nations of the control of their societies. At its worst, neoliberalism is a threat to democracy and leads to exploitation. (22)

Jack Welch, former CEO of General Electric and Fortune Magazine is a symbol of neoliberalism in action. Once Welch became CEO of GE, he shuttered plants and laid off huge numbers of workers even though GE was profitable, and the economy was healthy. Welch's cuts were not just to ensure corporate profitability. He implemented "lean production" to maximize shareholder value. His philosophy was efficiency for the sake of efficiency. Welch eliminated the jobs of at least a quarter of GE's employees. Of course, the previous crisis had conditioned labor and unions to just accept that cuts had to be made. We workers always must make sacrifices, but we never seem to be in line for any of the rewards. (23)

Some of you may remember a movie called Roger & Me filmed by Michael Moore. At the time of the film, Roger Smith had reduced the number of Flint employees from 80,000 in 1978 to 50,000 in 1992. (24, 25) As of 2015, GM had less than 8,000 employees in Flint. (26) When Reagan visited Flint, he suggested the workers move across the country to find jobs. I don't remember Reagan offering to help these workers to relocate. GM flew in Pat Boone to tell everyone what a standup guy Roger Smith was. Boone was sure to reassure everyone that everything would turn out fine. I can assure you that Flint never recovered. No one ever offered to help the displaced workers find new work. Everyone assumed that it would just work out. Those who didn't adapt weren't considered victims of Roger Smith. Those who failed must have deserved their fate. The most disturbing part is how many people were okay with what was happening. In the film, the Flint plant was having a going away party. A few minutes into the footage, one of the workers yells at everyone that they need to wake up because they are all losing their jobs. Why were they having a party?

It seems to me that reducing taxes for the wealthy creates a perverse incentive. If you decrease the taxes for the decision makers, they are more inclined to cut costs by cutting jobs and wages. By letting the wealthy keep more profits, they have more to gain by 'lean operations'. If the wealthy were taxed more, then they wouldn't have so much to gain from maximizing profit. Why not just pay the workers fairly? I will give you an example of a perverse incentive. Hanoi, Vietnam once had a rat problem. So, the French decided they would pay for every rat tail they received. The program worked well at first. But then the colonials discovered that the locals began farming rats so that they could turn in the tails for the bounties. Hanoi had even more rats after the program than before. This is also a problem with Key Performance Indicators (KPI's). You can never tell when the consequences of a program will deviate from its intended goal. (27)

Financial crashes, climate change and even President Trump's victory may be the final result of neoliberalism. Neoliberalism would have each of us competing with each other. According to John Nash's Game Theory, a group does better when it cooperates to ensure that each member gets a fair share. In the Prisoner's Dilemma, the group does better if each member agrees to keep quiet and receive a reduced sentence. But if one member sells out the others, they can go free. But the rest of the group gets the maximum sentence. In a cartel, each group can be assured to get a set amount if they stick together. But if one member breaks the agreement, they gain while the other members lose. John Nash's theory shows that the group does better when the members cooperate. Everyone wins something. But without an agreement, we must spend time and resources competing. There are a few winners and many losers. (28) According to neoliberalism, any government intervention is considered an attack on liberty. The government should reduce taxes and regulations. Unions and collective bargaining should be curtailed. (29)

The worst part is that each of us internalize this nonsense. We are being brainwashed. The rich persuade themselves that they are all self-made. The poor are blamed and even criminalized. If the system is working against you, just figure it out. According to neoliberalism, the poor don't deserve our help. If you have a business failure, medical catastrophe, or a stroke of bad luck; it must be your fault. There is no reason to have a social safety net. Social programs are for the lazy. The truth is that we are all vulnerable. Bad things happen to good people. Neoliberalism doesn't recognize that. Milton Friedman stated that being a monopoly would be considered a reward for efficiency. While the Republicans are best known as neoliberals, even the democrats have bought into this philosophy. Bill Clinton signed NAFTA into law in 1992. NAFTA was a significant step in the globalization of our economy. (30)

Neoliberalism states that we can exercise choice by voting with our dollars. Of course, the wealthy have a lot more 'votes'. Never mind "one man, one vote". When the people feel disenfranchised by the system, they will do anything for a change. Fascist movements build their base from the disenfranchised. I worry that we may lose our democracy and capitalism if we are swept away in a blind push for reform. (29)

According to neoliberals, no one person or group can manage the economy. The market is a type of sorting algorithm that determines prices and values of each good. The market becomes a kind of giant computer. All management is left to the market to decide. Government intervention is left out. The only outcome involves the bottom line. Values have no place in business. (30) Personally, I worry about unsupervised algorithms. Artificial Intelligence is the field where algorithms are used to replicate human thought. Artificial Intelligence (AI) uses complicated formulas to sort through vast amounts of data. The market algorithm reminds me of an AI experiment. Some experiments into AI have yielded results that are racist, sexist, and biased. (31) It seems that the AI models perpetuate biases that were unintentionally input. An algorithm will yield the same results as before. This is where we are headed. This is the result of unchecked algorithms. If we continue with the same systems, we can expect even more inequality in the future.

Milton Friedman – Capitalism and Freedom

In 1962, Milton Freidman wrote Capitalism and Freedom. (32) Friedman is considered one of the fathers of modern neoliberalism. To understand our current economy, it is important to review Friedman's writings. Capitalism and freedom both sound like ideals. How can you have too much freedom? But we need government intervention to ensure that individuals are protected from those with economic power.

Friedman notes that the burden of government should be as small as possible. It is better to have governing control locally than nationally. If you don't like what happens in a city, it is much easier to move to another city than it is to another country. (Friedman, pp 2-3) I agree with both ideas. We don't want the government just to have rules. Nor do we want taxes for the sake of paying taxes. If a regulation is a needless barrier to business, we should throw it out. An example might be a requirement to have a business license where the sole purpose is to provide fees to the government. You shouldn't have any more government or taxes than what is needed. But what is needed? We must have sufficient defenses, infrastructure, healthcare, education, and public works. The government must spend to adequately provide what the citizens need. Friedman notes that no great advancement has been produced by the government. He must not have been aware that NASA oversaw designing and launching satellites. (33) He can be forgiven for not knowing that the Department of Defense developed the Internet. The Internet did not gain widespread recognition until the 1990s. (34)

Friedman disapproves of the 'welfare state' where our government provides in order to have equality and welfare. (Friedman p.5) He seems to believe that those with money will voluntarily see to the needs of their poor neighbors. Friedman tells us to beware 'democratic socialism'. (Friedman, p. 7) We shouldn't become outright socialists. We don't need the government to run businesses. The government should not try to plan the economy. But we do need guardrails. We need laws to ensure the liberty and rights of the workers. We need to tax appropriately so that the wealthy pay their fair share. Friedman argues that for us to be free, we must have a free market. He even admits that we can't have absolute freedom. (Friedman, pp. 25-26) While the government should not run the economy, they must limit the ability of the wealthy to infringe on the rights of the workers. Friedman warns us that we do not want those in government to be our masters. But we don't want those with money to be our masters either. Friedman says that if one employer doesn't pay enough, we can find another. But what if all employers are the same and none of them pay enough for the worker to support their family?

Friedman states that discrimination shouldn't happen in a free-market economy because minorities are anonymous. (Friedman, p. 21) What about the occasions where the customers or vendors are known? On page 109, he suggests that the free-market economy makes us all equal. The text suggests that since we can all own property, the free market prevents discrimination. This does not match what we know about the history of civil rights in our country. Did he not see any 'Whites only' signs in the 60s? Friedman is missing the point. People of color did not receive any protections or civil rights from the free-market economy. Minorities were able to enter the free-market economy because of protections legislated by the government in response to the civil-rights movement.

Friedman would have us remove minimum wages, the Interstate Commerce Commission, the Federal Communications Commission, and even the Social Security programs. He supports removing the draft in peacetime, but he said nothing about war. (Friedman, pp 35-36) Why do we need a draft in peacetime? He would have us work for pennies a day for the rest of our lives while our children listen to f-bombs over the public radio.

Friedman notes that businesses have no other social responsibility beyond serving the interest of the stockholders. (Friedman, p 133) This is how businesses operate. This is the same rationale used by corporations to lay off thousands of their workers. Perhaps they have a right to do whatever they want. We also have the right to not buy from companies who don't treat their workers fairly. While business may only care about making money, our government is responsible for looking out for OUR interests!

Final Thoughts

I would say that it was a mistake to abandon using Keynesian policies in favor of neoliberalism. I believe that the crisis in the 1970's was caused by massive public debt that caused the devaluation of our currency. The devaluation and oil shocks caused inflation that shut down the economy. The oil shocks were unavoidable. But we should have continued having the government provide jobs and build infrastructure while being more conservative about cutting taxes.

Pope Francis had this to say about trickle-down economics. "Some people continue to defend trickle-down theories which assume that economic growth, encouraged by a free market, will inevitably succeed in bringing about greater justice and inclusiveness in the world. This opinion, which has never been confirmed by the facts, expresses a crude and naive trust in the goodness of those wielding economic power and in the sacralized workings of the prevailing economic system. Meanwhile, the excluded are still waiting." (35)

Next, we will review the economic policies since the 1960s that have shaped our current economic world.

———

ECONOMIC HISTORY FROM 1960 TO 2000: THE BEGINNING OF OUR PROBLEMS

ECONOMIC HISTORY FROM 1960 TO 2000: THE BEGINNING OF OUR PROBLEMS

John F. Kennedy (JFK)

In 1962, John F. Kennedy announced his plans for permanent tax cuts for individuals and corporations. This is considered a supply-side tactic, and it worked! These tax cuts resulted in a 106-month economic expansion that wasn't seen again until the 1990s. Real GDP growth averaged 5%. Previously, the GDP grew by over 2%. U.S. Payrolls increased and government tax revenues grew by 65%. (1) I usually advocate demand-side tactics, but Kennedy's plan was successful. How can this be? These tax cuts were so successful because the highest marginal corporate tax rate was 52% and the highest marginal income tax rate was 91%. That's right, 91%! FDR considered raising the highest individual rate to 100%. This sounds insane to me. George Romney turned down several bonuses because most of his extra earnings would be paid in taxes. He wouldn't keep even a dime of every extra dollar he earned. (2) I believe that we should tax the rich more. We need to rebuild our infrastructure, repair our social safety net, and reduce our deficit. I don't think that we should punish the rich for having money. Our tax goals may be best demonstrated by the Laffer curve. Arthur Laffer noted that the government would collect zero revenue at 0% tax rate. If we taxed the revenue at 100%, there would be no economy to tax. But there is a summit where the optimal tax rate leads to the optimal tax revenue. If we tax less than the optimal rate, we are missing out on potential tax revenue. If we tax more than the optimal rate, we create a drag on the economy that causes us to lose revenue even though we tax at a higher rate. (3) I think that we can all agree that a 91% tax rate is too high. It's difficult to pinpoint the exact amount of taxes that are optimum. I believe our current top tax rates are too low.

Kennedy lowered interest rates to keep the economy growing. (4) In 1961, Kennedy was able to raise the minimum wage to $1.25 per hour. This may not sound like much in today's dollars, but it is important to regularly adjust the minimum wage for inflation. (5)

Lyndon Johnson (LBJ)

While the 1960s tax cuts were planned by Kennedy, the bill was passed after Kennedy's death under President Johnson. President Johnson declared a 'War on Poverty' to build his 'Great Society'. He also drastically increased our role in the Vietnam War.

Johnson passed a great deal of legislation to bring about the Great Society. His goals included ending poverty, reducing crime and inequality, and improving the environment. Some of his programs were intended to develop job skills and provide job training. Johnson started the Medicare and Medicaid program in 1964. These programs provided healthcare for the elderly and the poor. The Food Stamp Act of 1964 provided coupons for the poor that could only be used to purchase food items. (6) Another program was the Housing and Urban Development Act of 1965. This program provided federal funding for urban renewal and development. Access to home mortgages and rent subsidy programs were provided for Americans who qualified. (7) The poverty rate dropped from over 20% in 1960 to approximately 13% by 1970. (8)

Our welfare system began in 1935 as part of the New Deal package. Our unemployment insurance system also started with the New Deal. The most contentious program might be the Aid to Families with Dependent Children program. The original intent was to provide cash payments to families with children who had no means to support themselves. In 1965, Congress passed the Public Welfare Amendments to improve public assistance and child welfare services. There is a debate as to whether this is a program that helps those in need or if it subsidizes laziness. (9) This debate was one of the key topics in Reagan's presidential campaign in 1980. Our welfare system had some vulnerabilities to being abused.

While President Johnson aimed for a legacy for helping the poor, he is most remembered for the Vietnam War. Our role in Vietnam drastically increased during Johnson's presidency. Kennedy sent over support while Nixon ordered the withdrawal from Vietnam. The Vietnam War was one of the longest and costliest wars the U.S. had fought. Much of this budget involved the development of new technologies. The budget for this war peaked at $85 billion in 1969. (10, 11)

The Vietnam War and the War on Poverty cost the U.S. a lot of money. Since Johnson spent so much money, the federal deficit grew out of control. The tax cuts that were enacted actually increased government revenue. But there is a limit to how much we can spend. We were on the gold standard until the 1970s. Once the deficit reached a certain level, the U.S. did not have enough gold to cover all the debt. When we withdrew from the gold standard, the value of our dollar dropped. This was one of the reasons we had such high inflation in the 1970s. (12)

Richard Nixon and Gerald Ford

One of Nixon's chief accomplishments was opening relations with China. Prior to Nixon's 1972 visit, China had been an isolated country for at least 25 years. Nixon's intent was to gain another ally against Russia. It might be hard for Nixon to imagine the amount of trade that has occurred between the two nations since then. For good or bad, it was Nixon's visit that allowed trade with China to begin. China's economy has grown by leaps and bounds since trade has resumed. No one could foresee how many jobs we would create for China at the expense of American jobs. (13)

In 1971, Nixon declared drug abuse to be public enemy number one. He created the Drug Enforcement Agency (DEA) as well as several other agencies to battle drugs. Reagan would eventually up the ante of the War on Drugs to the level it was in the 1980s. During Reagan's presidency, minimum sentencing laws were enacted. Since a higher percentage of drug users were minorities, inequality for those incarcerated increased. We have since relaxed many of the sentencing standards and enforcement of the drug laws. But drugs and incarceration for minorities remain big problems. (14)

In the 1970s, the U.S. had to wrestle with high inflation and low growth. In 1971, Nixon imposed a 90-day price and wage freeze. He imposed a 10% import tax and removed the dollar from the gold standard. Many believe that these actions caused the stagflation that the U.S. suffered in the 1970s. Interest rates were raised to historically high levels that would only increase in the 1980s.

(15, 16) In 1973, Arab members of OPEC placed an embargo on the U.S. because we supported Israel during the Arab Israeli War. The price of oil quadrupled during this period. (17)

After the Watergate Scandal caused Nixon to resign in 1974, Gerald Ford was sworn in as president. His plan to combat inflation involved Whip Inflation Now (WIN) buttons. We would wear these buttons to remind people not to spend as much. Businesses were asked to voluntarily resist raising prices even if it meant operating at a loss. Ford lost to President Carter in the election of 1976. (18)

Our problems were caused by overspending, the devaluation of the U.S. dollar, sharp increases in the price of oil, and ineffective government response. Wage and price freezes are an example of government overreach. It's as difficult to determine the line between government protection and overreach as it is to determine the tax rate that will provide the optimal tax revenues. While the minimum wage laws protect workers from being unfairly paid, price controls seem to be measures that put artificial restrictions on the market. Perhaps the government tried too hard to keep inflation down. Inflation would be the natural result of a weaker U.S. dollar and an increase in the price of oil.

Jimmy Carter

In 1977, Jimmy Carter was sworn in as President. Carter's term was plagued by inflation. The rate of inflation rose from 6% in 1976 to more than 12 percent in 1980. Unemployment had reached 7.5%. The economic problems were partly due to the country's energy problems. Carter attempted to form a new energy program, but it did not pass the Senate. (19) Oil prices rose rapidly from 1979 to 1980. The Iranian Revolution caused a reduction in Iran's oil output. While Iran's reduction only caused a 7% reduction of the world oil production, the situation caused fears about further disruptions in the supply of oil. (20) In response to the earlier energy crisis, Carter formed the Department of Energy. (21) He also created the Department of Education. (22) He attempted to pass a universal healthcare plan, but that measure didn't pass. (23) In 1978, Carter signed the Airline Deregulation Act. This act removed government control over fares, routes, and market entry for new airlines. This was the first step in a long line of deregulation. (24) While Carter was able to form several new federal organizations, he was not able to effectively improve the economy. His inability to work with Congress prevented him from making any real changes. He was too much of an outsider in Washington. (25) With the economic problems that plagued the 1970s, the nation needed a drastic change. Carter lost when he faced Reagan in the 1980 election.

Ronald Reagan

Reagan campaigned on steep tax cuts, increased defense spending, a balanced budget, and a constitutional amendment to ban abortion. Reagan promised to reform welfare too. In August 1981, the national union of air traffic controllers went on strike. Since federal union members were forbidden by law from striking, Reagan refused to negotiate. He gave them 48 hours to return to work. When the workers refused, he fired them. The public generally reacted positively to Reagan's solution to this dilemma. (26) Reagan usually followed the 'supply-side' economic policies. He proposed tax cuts of up to 30 percent in individual and corporate income tax rates. He hoped to follow Kennedy's tax cuts that stimulated the economy, increased economic growth, and increased tax revenues. Reagan was able to lower the highest individual tax rate from 70% to 50%. He proposed increasing military spending by $1.5 trillion while cutting social welfare programs such as education, food stamps, low-income housing, school lunches for poor children, Medicaid, and Aid to Families with Dependent Children. In 1982, a severe recession pushed the nation's unemployment rate to almost 11 percent. Reagan's policies caused the deficit to rise to $2.5 trillion. In response to the record deficit, he supported a $98.3 billion tax increase in 1982. (26) Reagan's policies added 40 million jobs, eased inflation, and drastically reduced unemployment. Still, there are reasons to believe that the tax cuts and economic growth benefited the wealthy at the expense of the poor. This was the beginning of our neoliberal decline for the middle class. (27)

Reagan's tax cuts led to a net reduction in tax revenue, especially in the first couple of years. He lowered the highest individual rate from 70% to 50%. It seems that Reagan managed to transverse the Laffer curve even after his later tax increases. Taxes may have been too high before, but now it seems that they may have been too low. The U.S. Federal Tax Revenue as a percentage of GDP decreased from 18.5% to 17.4% from 1980 to 1990. By slashing taxes for the wealthy, Reagan missed opportunities to keep spending programs that helped the poor and reduce the deficit. One great consequence for Reagan's tax reform was that the tax brackets became annually adjusted for inflation. Previously, inflation caused middle class families to reach higher tax brackets resulting in higher taxes. Reagan's tax plan created the largest tax reform the country had ever seen.

(28, 29, 30) One would think that Reagan's tax cuts for the wealthy would be more than what was necessary. And yet all future tax cuts included the most drastic cuts for the top brackets.

Reagan promised to increase military spending and he was true to his word. But those were different times. At that time, we feared nuclear annihilation and attack from communist countries. Reagan's foreign policy helped to defeat the U.S.S.R. and end the Cold War. It is good to have some government spending because that can provide good paying jobs and investments in research. (26)

In my research, I did not find any issues with our infrastructure until after Reagan's presidency. Although some investments could have been made in new infrastructure such as public transportation. Reagan did make budget cuts to the Environmental Protection Agency and the Department of Transportation. Reagan did not sign any laws that would reduce fuel consumption. Ford signed the Energy Policy and Conservation act in 1975 in response to the previous oil shock. The Department of Transportation set the first vehicle standards for gas mileage in 1978. It was during the 1980s that we began to see more fuel-efficient cars. Before then, cars were much larger and heavier. (31)

One of Reagan's goals was to reduce federal spending on social programs. He planned to revert funding for these programs to the states and cities. Before Reagan submitted his proposed budget, he had to remove the Social Security programs from the cutting board. But he was able to tighten enforcement for disabled recipients on Social Security. This ended benefits for more than a million people. These days, it seems that you must be completely bed bound to qualify for disability benefits. Means tested programs survived with moderate cuts, but other targeted programs such as jobs training programs, were removed entirely. (27)   While Reagan promised to end the system that made 'welfare queens', Bill Clinton made the most reforms to welfare.

Reagan slashed Medicaid spending by 18 percent. The spending for Health and Human Services was cut by 25 percent.   Many lost benefits such as reduced-price school lunches, Medicaid, and food stamps. From 1982 to 1987, unintended pregnancy rates increased by nearly 8 percent. Fifteen percent of the population lacked health insurance. (32)   Our rugged individualist, "get tough" on the poor approach is not working. People need help. The homeless population skyrocketed during Reagan's presidency. Homelessness is a complicated issue. Carter had signed the Mental Health Systems Act of 1980 that would provide grants to community mental health centers. Reagan voted to repeal that Act the next year. (33)   One of Reagan's plans was to allow patients in state psychiatric hospitals to leave if they wished.   His policy was that a person can only be committed involuntarily if they were a danger to themselves or others. Previously, a family member could have someone committed if they could convince a doctor that it was necessary. Reagan's policy gave more rights to those with mental health issues by allowing them to have more control of their treatment. There were many reports of psychiatric patients being abused in the past, so Reagan wanted to address those abuses. Once Reagan's policies were put into place, many of the inmates voted with their feet and left. So, once the hospitals emptied, they were closed. The problem is that we had these people with mental disabilities pouring out into the streets with no support systems. These people needed help in their transition to the outside world, and Reagan's policies failed them. They needed help, not budget cuts. Some people can't make life transitions without help. This is true whether it is leaving a mental hospital or getting a new job after being laid off. Yet Reagan cut job training programs. Rather than being tax paying citizens, some people just became homeless. The best solution to homelessness would be to set them up with a secure place to stay. Give the homeless access to medical care so that they can receive needed medication. But Reagan cut the housing and healthcare budgets. Many shelters sprang up, but these shelters have several problems. They are overcrowded and people feel that they lose their autonomy in these places. They feel that they are treated like animals in the crowded shelters, so they stay outside. The homeless feel like they have control on the outside. On the outside, they can keep their pets and hang out with their friends. Since shelters are more like warehouses, they fail to provide a safe personal space. These are the reasons that many prefer to avoid shelters. If the homeless could have a safe, secure, quiet personal space, then they would accept those spaces. Instead, we have people living on the outside with no access to the medications that would help them to fit into society. (34,35,36)

Another problem was Reagan's war on education. Reagan campaigned that he would shut down the Federal Department of Education that Carter had established. But once he met stiff resistance from Congress, he abandoned that plan. (37) We may have Reagan to blame for our massive student debt. Reagan was the governor of California during the Vietnam War. Many of the war protests happened on college campuses. Reagan developed a distaste for college educated liberals during his tenure as governor. As governor, he cut state spending for California's public universities. After all, we wouldn't want our workers to become too educated. They might then question all the tax cuts we give to the rich. Reagan slashed spending on higher education by 25 percent from 1980 to 1985. (38) In Adam Smith's The Wealth of Nations, Smith states that skilled labor is the most valuable resource that a nation can have. One can imagine that an educated labor force would only make our nation more prosperous. But having equal education might upset our current class system. By funding our future generations' college educations, we are funding a valuable resource for the country and for our children. Those who are educated make more money. This money can be taxed. So public funding of education should provide payoffs in the future that will pay both our children and the future government. In 1944, the U.S. passed the GI Bill that provided free tuition for 8 million veterans. Edward Humes noted that the GI Bill gave our nation 14 Nobel Prize winners, 3 Supreme Court Judges, 3 presidents, and millions of other professionals. In 1952, the nation spent $7 billion dollars and received extra taxes of $12.8 billion over the next 40 years. Our educated nation led the world in innovation. Before the 1980s, it is estimated that states paid 65 percent of college costs, federal aid covered 15 percent, and the student had to take on 20 percent. Now, students need massive student loans to cover 80 percent of education costs. In many European countries, higher education is completely provided by the government. (39)

Reagan was known as the great deregulator. Some regulations were good, some harmed the economy. If a regulation serves to hinder businesses with no gain to the public, it should be removed. For instance, a business fee collected by the government that hinders operation, should be removed. Taxing profits on business is different because unprofitable businesses aren't affected. An example of a regulation that only limits growth would be the airline's regulations. Reagan allowed the airlines to manage their own schedules and fees. (40)   In 1982, Reagan approved the Germain Depository Institutions Act.   This act allowed savings and loans to offer more risky products, expanded lending authority and reduced regulatory oversight.   This reduced oversight also led to more lax accounting rules. These deregulations allowed the Savings and Loan Crisis to occur. (41)

Our response to the economic disaster of the 1970s was to abandon the demand side policies that worked so well before. It wasn't that the Keynesian approach was flawed. The economic problems were caused by overspending and a shift in international factors that affected the U.S. economy. We need the government to add to demand and provide public goods that can't be done by private organizations. We didn't need the government to take total control, but we still needed guard rails. Reagan didn't create our economic situation single-handedly. But he did start us on a path that led from the decline from the Golden Age of Capitalism to the bloody economic free-for-all that we have today.

George H.W. Bush Sr.

George Bush Sr. was known more for is foreign policy than his successes on the economy. In August of 1990, Saddam Hussein invaded Kuwait. In 1991, the U.S. entered the Gulf War. (42, Greene pp. 139-141)

For 1992 & 1993, Bush raised the top earning tax rate from a historic low of 28% to 31% to close the spending gap and reduce the federal deficit. (43) This wasn't a drastic tax increase, but it may have damaged his standing with conservatives and the public. (Greene, pp. 104-106) This conflicted with his pledge "Read my lips. No new taxes", but the tax increases and spending cuts allowed the federal government to have budget surpluses in the 1990s.

George Bush Sr. started the process for the adoption of the North American Free Trade Agreement known as NAFTA. NAFTA was signed in December of 1992 after Bush lost reelection, but Clinton won ratification in 1993. (Greene, pp. 222-223, 44) NAFTA had a massive impact on wages, jobs, and U.S. economic growth.

Bush Sr. was troubled by a mild recession in 1990. The unemployment rate rose from 5.9 percent in 1989 to 7.8 percent in mid-1991. This was one of the factors that caused him to lose to Clinton in 1992. (45) One catch phrase of Clinton's campaign was 'it's the economy, stupid." (46) Another factor would be the campaign of Ross Perot. He was a Texas billionaire who ran as an independent. He was the only candidate who crusaded against NAFTA. He also wanted to tackle the federal debt. At some points, he led the polls. (47)

NAFTA & Globalization

NAFTA was signed by the U.S., Canada, and Mexico in 1992. It took effect in 1994. All tariffs within North America were immediately lifted. (48) Bill Clinton and his staff fully supported NAFTA. Clinton believed that free trade was best for the economy. (49) They believed that by including Mexico in NAFTA, they would be able to get Mexico to improve their standards and pay for workers so that they matched the U.S. and Canada. They wanted to 'raise the floor' of working standards. But Mexico did not make any improvements. One problem was that many jobs went to Mexico because the workers were paid less, and

Mexico had lower environmental standards. Robert Reich, formerly the U.S. Secretary of Labor, stated that it wasn't NAFTA that caused the most damage. It was the favored status to China that cost the U.S. the most jobs. The Economic Policy Institute (EPI) warned that NAFTA would lead to significant job losses. The EPI also warned that the TPP (Trans-Pacific Partnership) would lead to trade deficits, loss of U.S. jobs, and lower wages. The EPI was right on all predictions. (50, 51, 52, 53, 54) While Reich was part of Clinton's administration that ratified NAFTA, he notes that NAFTA and all subsequent trade deals have not worked out well for the American worker. The 1% manage to keep all their money because they send their money and ideas abroad. They make the products abroad, then they sell them abroad without any money coming back to the U.S. Since our trade agreements have no provisions for wage standards or environmental standards, companies send everything overseas to undercut American workers. (55) The EPI noted that NAFTA gave the shafta to workers in all three countries involved. Robert Scott estimated that NAFTA eliminated 766,000 jobs in manufacturing in the U.S. These displaced workers had to pick up lower paying service jobs. Somehow, those who run the factories in Mexico managed to ensure that the workers in Mexico wouldn't have any gains in their wages. Even workers in Canada took a hit for stable employment. (56) Why shouldn't we just raise our tariffs?

A tariff is a tax that a country places on goods imported from another country. It usually protects the businesses inside the country because it makes imports more expensive. If a consumer wants to buy an import, they must pay a higher price. High tariffs are called protectionist policies. This is good for businesses of the home country.

But this does lead to higher prices for consumers. Many economists feel that tariffs restrict free trade and slow down economic growth. It is risky to raise tariffs because it may lead to a trade war. This is where countries raise their tariffs in retaliation for a tariff increase. It is believed that unfair trade was a factor in the American Revolution. David Ricardo developed the idea of the comparative advantage. This theory maintains that if one country is better at producing one product, and a second country is better at producing a second product, then each country should do what they do best. Each country would then trade. With free trade, each country can produce goods at the lowest price. Tariffs create an interference with this arrangement. (57)

Free trade gained a lot of support because it was noted that the Smoot-Hawley Tariff Act of 1930 made the Great Depression worse. Many other countries raised their tariffs on American products in response. This caused more businesses to close. (58) While some economists now doubt the effect of the Smoot-Hawley Act on the Great Depression, it was most important that people thought that high tariffs can cause a downturn in the economy. Until Trump, most politicians have favored free trade.

After reviewing history, I have a new perspective on international trade. As it stands, our free trade agreements are leading to a race to the bottom. Since our trade agreements have no provisions for wage standards or environmental standards; companies can choose to exploit workers in countries who will allow the lowest possible wages and pollute as much as they want. The problem with our trade agreements is that there are NO strings attached. Clinton and his staff expected that Mexico would improve their standards. They did not. If countries were required to upgrade their standards, then there would not be such an advantage to offshoring jobs. There would not be such a demand for globalization because standards would be similar within the trading block. Standards in other countries would improve. We would even make progress on climate change. Currently, globalization represents exploitation of workers overseas and unemployment and exploitation for American workers. It is also killing our planet.

Bill Clinton

Bill Clinton ratified NAFTA in January 1994. This agreement set the precedent for the Trans-Pacific Partnership that would later be proposed by Obama. The Clinton's spent most of their first year in office to pass NAFTA. In 1993, Clinton gave China the most favored nation status and he minimized tariffs on Chinese goods. The original agreement would be dependent on human rights reform. But once again, the U.S. agreed to reduce tariffs with no strings attached. The hope was that China would be more democratic and buy our goods. But the only exports to China were our jobs. China never improved their human rights policies, nor did they make any occupational or environmental reforms. (59)

After NAFTA was passed, the Clintons turned their attention to healthcare. The healthcare reform bill went through many revisions, but the goal seemed to be a clone of the Obamacare bill that passed over 15 years later. Clinton wanted to include an individual mandate to purchase insurance just as Obama did. There would also be an exchange. Like Obamacare, Clinton's plan would remove the policy of not covering pre-existing conditions. One version included a market-based approach just like

Obamacare. But there was also a version that called for a single payer plan. The Clintons decided on offering a comprehensive package rather than a bare bones plan. There were many versions passed back and forth because it was difficult to get a consensus. Some took offense that Hillary Clinton was taking charge of healthcare reform since no one elected her. The measure failed to pass before the Republicans took control of Congress in 1994. The GOP managed to kill the reform and have Clinton bear the blame for its failure to pass. (60, 61)

There are several issues with the Clinton Plan and Obamacare. The first issue is the individual mandate. American citizens do not like to be told what to do. There is a difference between employment rules that protect workers from abusive companies and 'nanny' rules that are 'for our own good'. Many like to be responsible for themselves. How do you enforce the mandate? What about the homeless? For Clinton, how would you design an exchange before the Internet was adopted? Obamacare had the advantage that consumers could use the Internet to shop for providers. What happens if a person can't afford insurance because they are unemployed? Wouldn't it be better to create good paying jobs so that employers can provide insurance? Perhaps the employers could be required to provide insurance.

Another issue is a single payer system. Americans want choice. It is likely that the government would choose single payer. This would be a socialist overreach. While we do need governmental guard rails, it is better for competing companies to work to provide the best plan at reduced cost. Competing companies should provide more services for less. A government system is likely to become an inefficient bureaucracy. Many Americans wish to avoid the Universal

Healthcare System because they feel that they can't buy better service. A major objection is that Universal Health Care creates long wait times to receive care. One study showed that the median wait time in Canada between a referral from a general practitioner to a specialist is over 19 weeks. (62) The final issue has to do with cost. If we offer too much to everybody, how will we pay for everything? A comprehensive plan risks breaking the bank with excessive federal deficits. Costs are likely to be higher because of the lack of competition.

Perhaps a better plan would be to expand Medicaid. If a person makes less than a certain amount, they can receive a Medicaid card. The problem with mandates is that the poor are worst at compliance. While the homeless wouldn't have to pay any fees for violating the mandate, Obamacare risks leaving them out. We should have a system that automatically enrolls people in Medicaid if they cannot afford healthcare coverage. Hospitals could receive a 'finder's fee' for enrolling underserved patients. Employers should be required to provide healthcare. If you work full time, you should have your needs met. It seems likely that most people who do not work should qualify for Medicaid.

In 1993, Clinton attempted to pass a $16.3 billion stimulus package, but it was blocked by Congress. There was a lot of infighting between Clinton and Congress, especially after the Republicans took control of Congress after the midterm elections of 1994. The bill included $4 billion to extend unemployment, $3 billion to repair highways and bridges, $1.2 billion for public bus systems, $2.5 billion for community block grants for infrastructure, $1.2 billion for water treatment plants, $1 billion for public works, $1.9 million to provide Pell Grants for low and middle-income students, $1 billion for summer school for poor students, $1 billion for Job training programs, $1.1 billion for housing and immunization, and other programs. This program was blocked over concerns about the deficit. (63) This program was exactly what our country needed. Government spending on public projects is important for our infrastructure and it provides good paying jobs. As it is, our infrastructure started to crumble a few years after this bill was rejected. Clinton was trying to battle a jobless recovery after a recession. Congress did not do us any favors when they blocked this proposal.

In February 1993, Clinton passed the Family Medical Leave Act (FMLA). This act provides 12 weeks of job protection if the employee or a member of their family has a medical issue that requires them to leave work for an extended period. The employer must continue the employee's healthcare while they are on leave. While the employer is not required to pay the employee during their leave, this act protects an employee from losing their job because they need time off for a medical issue. (64)

In 1993, Clinton signed the Omnibus Budget Reconciliation Act of 1993. This law raised the top tax bracket from 31% to 39.6%. Business income tax rates were raised to 35%. The cap of wages taxed for Medicare was removed. Even the taxable portion of Social Security benefits were increased. All these tax increases except for Social Security would be expected to bring us to the optimal point on the Laffer curve. The tax increases served to reduce the deficit and create a budget surplus. In 1996, Clinton signed the Taxpayer Relief Act. The tiered capital gains taxes were lowered from 28% to 20% and 15% to 10%. An exemption on capital gains on the sale of a house was created at $250,000 for singles and $500,000 for married couples. The economy grew. In February 2000, the economy broke the record for the longest period of economic expansion. In 1997, Clinton created the State Children's Health Insurance Program (SCHIP). This program expanded the children eligible for Medicaid coverage by raising the income levels that would disqualify coverage for children. The Roth IRA (Individual Retirement Account) was also created in 1997. (65, 66, 67) While the Roth IRA helps individuals to save for retirement, this act marked a transition from employer sponsored retirement plans to individual retirement plans. The beginning of this transition started when 401k programs started in the 1980s. Previously, companies set aside money and managed the pension in a pool. The employers took responsibility for caring for employees once they were ready to retire. Once 401k and Roth IRA accounts were started, the employers convinced the workers that pensions no longer made sense. Now, the workers must set aside a portion of their own money for retirement. (68) This amounts to a pay cut. Previously, employers might set aside 5% of an employee's wages to invest in a combined pension account. Now, the employee must set aside the 5%. This assumes that the employees know how to invest. Pensions are safer because they are managed by professionals. Pensions are also insured by the Pension Benefit Guaranty Corporation (PBGC). If an employee invests poorly, then they will just work until they die. Another issue is saving enough money to prevent outliving your savings. With enough people, you can establish a risk pool so that you can determine the money you will need to cover the retirement responsibilities. But a single individual can never tell how long they will live. Perhaps the average life expectancy is 79. Under a pension, you would need to assume most people will live an average of 79 years. But what if you have a 401k and live to 89?

You are responsible for ensuring you don't run out of money before you turn 89. You must save even more because you can't manage risk for a single person. The consensus is that most workers do not have enough money saved to retire.

In 1999, Clinton signed the Financial Services Modernization Act. This act repealed the Glass-Steagall Act that separated consumer banking from investment banking. This act also loosened regulations on risky financial derivatives. This deregulation is credited with playing a factor in the Great Recession of 2008. (69)

In 1996, Clinton signed The Personal Responsibility and Work Opportunity Reconciliation Act. This law ended the AFDC program and replaced it with the Temporary Aid to Needy Families (TANF) program. As its name says, TANF is temporary. It only allows a maximum of 5 years of payments to an individual. All able-bodied adults that were aged 18-49 must be working or in job training. Management of the programs were referred to the state. These states sometimes had even more stringent requirements than the old AFDC. These laws did a great job of getting tough on the poor, but there weren't as many jobs programs as needed. (70)

Relief for the poor is a balancing act. The purpose should be to help those who can work become independent. But we want to make sure that those who can't find a job won't starve. Children are the ones most hurt by poverty. Having grown up on AFDC, I can tell you that living on welfare isn't easy. On welfare, families are committed to being poor. Welfare yields a fixed income. If you work, your income is whatever you can get someone to pay you. People on welfare always must prove that they need the money. With welfare comes intrusion and lack of privacy.

You must report any income you make. It really is better to have a decent paying job than to be on welfare. We must look at what we can afford. Everyone who isn't working is being supported. We can't support everyone. And when we give to the poor, we can't provide a middle-class life for them. Whether we provide health insurance or cash payments, we must provide the amount needed to prevent suffering. But we can't be extravagant because we can't afford to be. We must leave an incentive for adults to try to work if they are able.

The best law we can pass is to raise the minimum wage. This would help families to support themselves without needing government support. Employers should not lowball their employees and then suggest that those employees apply for benefits. Since cash benefits are temporary, a person can't work for a low paying employer for long without becoming permanently ineligible for benefits. What happens if a person is not disabled enough for disability, but they are still unemployable? Many laws make these assumptions that we just need to give people a boot to their behinds to get them to work. But the programs for job training are limited. We have cut financial aid for people to get an education. When companies shed thousands of jobs, we expect people to just figure it out for themselves.

If a person can work, then they are better off working than remaining on welfare. But there are many barriers to independence. Will jobs pay enough for people to support their families? This is a priority. Are there job training programs to help people get jobs that are open? For some families, reliable childcare is a huge barrier. Has enough been done to ensure that children are safe when parents are working? What happens when there are no relatives available to help with childcare? There are Earned Income Tax Credits.   Are they enough?   Workers need transportation. But we haven't done much to provide safe, reliable public transportation. Our society relies on cars, but cars are expensive. The insurance, car payments, gas and car repairs add up. What happens if a person is unemployable? Why would a person jump into the uncertainty of the job market when money is given to them? We can't keep people on welfare forever unless they are disabled. But we need to do more to help them. There is also what I call the welfare trap. I have had people ask why the poor can't get a part time job while drawing welfare. They can, to a point. After making a certain amount of money, the state reduces the amount they give you. Until you are independent of welfare, you don't make much money from working because your pay decreases the money the state gives you. If you aren't getting more money to work, why work?

      We need to make sure there are enough resources to help people make the transition to independence. A lot of our welfare reform was just shirking responsibility on to someone else. Clinton's policies may have yielded results in the good times when there were jobs, but our safety net came crashing down during the Great Recession. Clinton's plan didn't even adjust the grants to the states for inflation. So, when the hard times came, the states were short of funds.

CHAPTER SEVEN

———

OUR RECENT ECONOMIC HISTORY
(2001-2023)

OUR RECENT ECONOMIC HISTORY
(2001-2023)

George W. Bush

In 2001 and 2003, George W. Bush passed two rounds of tax cuts. Many of the tax cuts were aimed at the middle class. His reasoning was that since the government budget was in surplus, he should give some of the money back to the people. While the middle class benefited, the highest earners benefited the most. The top tax rate was lowered from 39.6% to 35%. These tax cuts were set to expire in 2010. Most of the tax cuts remained except for the rates for the top tier. The Bush Tax Cuts also reduced the capital gains rate and the taxes paid on dividends. The money for the top tax rates could have been spent on government programs or reducing the deficit. Instead, the national deficit doubled during Bush's presidency. We had two wars during Bush's presidency that caused the federal deficit to grow as it did. Military spending increased because of the two wars and Bush wanted to build up the military after Clinton's cuts. We increased spending and cut taxes at the same time. This is expected to increase our borrowing costs in the future. (1, 2, 3)

In 2006, Bush attempted to pass a plan that would increase border security, establish a guest worker program, and create a path to citizenship for twelve million undocumented workers living in the U.S. That plan failed to pass the House. Bush tried again in 2007, but the second time the bill failed to pass the Senate. (4) While we need to have secure borders, we should have an amnesty program for people who have been here for a long time. Those who have been here the longest have established their lives here. The original purpose for immigration control was to limit the number of people immigrating to the United States to compete for jobs. Given the risk of terrorist attack from non-citizens, border security is necessary for our safety.

In 2006, Bush expanded Medicare by adding a drug benefit program. He also passed the No Child Left Behind Act. This act was intended to bring up education standards of low-income families by providing funding to low-income schools. It also gave parents of students in poor performing schools the option to seek schooling elsewhere. But he vetoed the SCHIP program that would have expanded the healthcare benefits to low-income families. (5, 6, 7) He felt that the program would be a move toward socialized health care.

Bush also tried to privatize Social Security. (8) This is where privatization is not a good idea. Bush wanted to allow people to take a portion of their social security taxes to invest in private accounts. Most people think they are better at investing than they are. Having private citizens manage their own social security is like having them manage their own 401k accounts. Since moving from pensions to 401k accounts, most people are not prepared for retirement. As it is, over half of people surveyed felt they were not on track to retire comfortably. (9) Fortunately, Bush's plan to privatize didn't pass.

The Great Recession

The Great Recession started in December of 2007 and did not end until June 2009. In 2009, the GDP fell by 2.8% and unemployment reached a high of 10%. The U.S. economy lost 8.7 million jobs and the Dow Jones lost over half of its value during this time. Home prices fell almost 30% and six million households lost their homes. (10)

Deregulation of the banking industry was a major factor in the Great Recession. Banks were taking more risks, mortgages were easier to get, and there was less oversight. Banks were writing mortgages to people with bad credit. Then the banks packaged these loans to sell as subprime mortgages. Some products being offered included loans with no down payment, interest only mortgages and ARM loans. ARM loans stand for Adjustable-Rate Mortgages. I have personally had realtors try to convince me to take an interest only and/or ARM loan so I could buy a bigger house. Both products are bad ideas. With interest only payments, you never pay on principal unless you make extra payments. But realtors will try to convince you to take an interest only loan so that the lower payments will allow you to buy a bigger house that will yield the realtor a bigger commission. ARM loans lure you in with low interest rates tied to the current rates. But what happens when those rates rise? A couple of points raise of the interest rate can raise the mortgage payment by hundreds of dollars. Another trick banks offer are balloon payment loans. These loans have you making payments as if you will have the loan for 30 years, but they are due in 10 or 15 years. What happens when the loan is due, and you can't find a good rate to refinance? From 2004 to 2006, the U.S. Federal Reserve raised the federal funds rate from 1% to 5.25%. Many households found that they could not keep up with these higher payments, so they just walked away from their houses. The banks purchased Credit Default Swaps from investors. The investors didn't realize the risk they were assuming. When so many families walked away from their homes, the investors were not able to handle all the defaults. Many banks filed for bankruptcy. George Bush passed the Emergency Economic Stabilization Act of 2008 and $700 billion in government bailouts under the TARP program. (Troubled Asset Relief Program) Companies such as General Motors, JP Morgan, Citigroup, Bank of America, and Wells Fargo all received bailouts. The Federal Reserve had to bring the interest rate from 5.25% to almost 0%. In February 2009, President Obama passed the American Recovery and Reinvestment Act that totaled $789 billion dollars with $212 billion in tax cuts and $311 billion in infrastructure, education, and health care. Obama also passed an initiative to help troubled families refinance their homes to take advantage of lower rates. Congress passed the Dodd-Frank Wall Street Reform and Consumer Protection Act to regulate the banking industry. (11)

Barack Obama

On February 17, 2009, Barack Obama signed the American Recovery and Reinvestment Act in order to end the Great Recession. This Act was intended to jump-start the economy, create new jobs, help small businesses, and cut taxes for working families. The bill included $85 billion for public infrastructure, $138 billion for healthcare, $108 billion for schools and Pell Grants. Tax relief included withholding reductions, stimulus checks, child tax care credits and an $8,000 tax credit for first-time home buyers. (12)

Obama signed an order to reauthorize the State Children's Health Insurance Program to cover an additional four million children. (13) After the midterm elections in 2010, Obama signed a one-year reduction in payroll taxes for employees as part of the Tax Relief, Unemployment Insurance Reauthorization, and Job Creation Act of 2010. This act included many tax cuts and incentives to stimulate the economy. It also extended unemployment benefits. (14,15) He also added new Medicare taxes to the higher tax brackets. (16) These programs were intended to help struggling families after the Great Recession.

The last time the federal minimum wage was raised was in 2009 under President Obama. It was raised to $7.25 per hour. The latest proposed change in 2023 would increase the minimum wage to $17 per hour. The new legislation waiting to be passed is the Raise the Wage Act of 2023. (17) As of 2023, the last increase was fourteen years ago. This would be the longest amount of time between wage increases since the minimum wage was established in 1938. Previously, the minimum wage was raised at least once a decade. Sometimes the minimum wage was adjusted every other year. It looks like we abandoned the concept completely and now we are just waiting for inflation to make the minimum wage concept meaningless.

After the Great Recession, the U.S. government needed to respond to the lax regulations and heavy risk taking that helped to cause the banks to fail. Senator Christopher J. Dodd and Rep. Barney Frank sponsored the Dodd-Frank Act to prevent another banking catastrophe. This act set new guidelines for the oversight of big banks, established the Consumer Financial Protection Bureau, and made the lending process more transparent to consumers. It also established the Volcker Rule to limit the risks that banks can take in investing and raised the amount that commercial banks had to carry in cash. Trump would later work to repeal provisions of the Dodd Frank Act in 2018. (18)

In 2015, Obama approved the Trans-Pacific Partnership (TPP). This agreement would lower tariffs for eleven countries including Australia, Brunei, Canada, Chile, Japan, Malaysia, Mexico, New Zealand, Peru, Singapore, and Vietnam. The Speaker of the House Mitch McConnell stated that they would not consider voting on the deal until after the elections. When Donald Trump entered office, he vetoed the TPP. (19) These agreements tend to lead to the U.S. losing jobs because the other countries have lower wage and environmental standards. When our leaders make these agreements, they don't make the favorable trade terms dependent on raising wages. So, these agreements act as a loophole for companies to pay workers less and pocket the money.

One of Obama's plans was to tax the wealthy. He did raise some taxes on the higher earners in 2013 by allowing the top tax rate to revert to 39.6 percent. A study published by AP News shows that the tax increases didn't hurt the economy or even the rich. The wealthy's share of the income stayed the same. Obama's increases were a step in the right direction. But raising taxes can be difficult. Many people believe that we should lower taxes just on principle. It would be prudent to raise taxes in increments so that we can see the effect those increases have on the economy. Data from other countries suggests that we would have to have top tax rates of 60 percent to reduce the wealthy's share of income. Perhaps 60 percent would be the optimal tax rate on the Laffer Curve. Top tax rates were 50 percent under Reagan. (20) One thing is certain. The wealthy don't need any more tax cuts.

OBAMACARE

On March 23, 2010, Barack Obama signed into law the Affordable Care Act (ACA) known as Obamacare. The most unpopular portion of this plan was the individual mandate. There were also concerns that the cost of the insurance plan would cause our deficit to balloon. (21, 22) Even with the Internet, the health exchange had many technical difficulties. Healthcare.gov would often lag and had problems with crashing during online applications. The use of multiple contractors for different aspects of the system caused a lack of compatibility in the different components. (23) The technical difficulties show a fundamental flaw in government spending. The government has a reputation for inefficiency and waste. This is why we need a separation of market goods from public goods. The government tends to be less efficient than private enterprise because it does not face competition or profitability concerns. For market goods, capitalism provides better results than socialism. But for public goods, we must be sure that those in charge provide what the public needs. Public goods need government oversight. We shouldn't buy public goods such as infrastructure, healthcare, poverty relief or justice at the lowest cost. The public needs sometimes transcend the bottom line. It may be that to provide what is needed, we will have to tolerate some government inefficiency. The government reputation for waste is overstated. You may have heard that the Pentagon once spent $600 to buy a hammer. But it turns out that the price for the hammer was exaggerated due to sloppy overhead allocation. The actual hammer cost $15. But every item had the same markup applied whether it was an aircraft engine or a hammer. (24).

Occupy Wall Street

The Occupy Wall Street movement lasted from September 17 to November 15, 2011. The 99% had finally had enough. The movement started in Zuccotti Park but quickly spread to other cities such as Washington D.C. (25) The slogan was 'We are the 99%." This referred to the income inequality between the wealthiest 1% and everyone else. (26) The people were protesting corporate influence on democracy, Wall Street practices that caused the Great Recession, and increasing inequality in wealth. (27) Some of the goals included less influence of corporations, more equality in wealth, more and better jobs, forgiveness of student loan debt, and reduction in foreclosures. (28) The largest issue with the movement was a lack of a clear set of demands. Occupy wanted to include as many people as possible, but there was no clear plan for change. Because there wasn't a clear agenda, the movement was not able to make any changes. (29) I can't wait for Occupy Wall Street 2.0. For the next time, we will need a clear agenda, clear demands, and a plan for making change. We will need to get organized.

Obama's Competition

The Presidential Campaign of John McCain (2008)

McCain planned to continue the Bush tax cuts, including the tax cuts for the wealthy. Lower taxes sound good, but our taxes for the wealthy are already too low. He pledged to eliminate pork-barrel spending, freeze nondefense spending, and reduce Medicare growth. (30) Reducing waste is a good goal, but how would he reduce spending and Medicare growth? What would he have to do to accomplish these cuts? He wanted to cut spending. But what programs would be cut? McCain did support cutting major military projects. (31) We need to be intentional in our spending and our budget cuts. We need to cut programs that don't help us, but we shouldn't cut needed programs just to make budget cuts. McCain supported NAFTA and free trade but without the strings attached to improve workers' rights. (32) He believed that protectionism comes at a heavy price. (33) But making conditions to lower tariffs isn't protectionism. We can have free trade with countries that honor workers' rights. Without accountability, free trade can provide a loophole where companies can get cheap labor to undercut our standard of living and avoid the laws, we have made to protect the workers and the environment. He believed in partial privatization of Social Security. (34) McCain's record on deregulation of bans is mixed. He voted for the Gramm-Leach-Bliley Act that loosened regulations on banks, brokerage houses, and insurance companies. He voted for the Sarbanes-Oxley Act that strengthened financial reporting requirements for publicly held companies, but he later expressed regret. (35, 36) McCain did not believe in the minimum wage. He voted against raising the minimum wage

19 times and even voted for legislation that would allow employers to pay less than the federal minimum wage if the state set a lower minimum. (37, 38, 39) I could not find that McCain had an aggressive plan to get the economy on track after the Great Recession.

The Presidential Campaign of Mitt Romney (2012)

In 2021, Senator Romney voted to pass a $1.2 trillion bipartisan bill to build our infrastructure. (40) In 1994, he advocated spending limits on congressional campaigns and abolishing political action committees. But in 2007, he criticized the McCain-Feingold Law. (41) We should limit the amount of influence that the wealthy have on politics. But our leaders need to be consistent in their principles. Romney argued that the federal government should pay for medicines for seniors through Medicare. But he pledged to raise the minimum age for Medicare eligibility for future seniors. (42, 43) Romney called for tying raises in the federal minimum wage to an indicator such as the rate of inflation. But when it came time to raise the minimum wage from $7.25 per hour to $10 per hour, he said that it wasn't a good time to raise the wage. (44) As Governor in 2003, Romney approved of the stimulus package that Obama passed. But during his campaign, he criticized the package. He didn't endorse the Bush tax cuts until his presidential campaign. (45, 46) We needed the stimulus package to get out of the Great Recession.

Romney believed in a balanced budget amendment to the Constitution. He also believed that we should have a debt ceiling contingent on major cuts and caps on spending. (47) But this leaves no room for stimulus packages if there is an emergency like a Great Recession or pandemic.

Romney stated that the excessive regulation is harming America's economy. (48) He promised to repeal the Dodd-Frank Wall Street Reform and Consumer Protection Act. He wanted to replace them with more streamlined regulations. (49) But would more streamlined regulations be sufficient? Removing regulations was a factor that caused the Great Recession. When asked how he would help with the housing and foreclosure problems, he stated that it would be best to not stop the foreclosure process and let it run its course. He went as far as to say that investors could salvage the property values and move people back into their homes as renters. (50) Romney believed that if he just reduced the regulations on businesses and cut taxes, the economy would create 12 million jobs. (51) Romney supported free trade, including NAFTA and the Trans-Pacific Partnership. (52) He favored getting tough with China to eliminate the Trade Deficit and would impose tariffs if needed. (53) He favored an individual 'savings account' for unemployment. He would also have a tax credit for those hiring long unemployed workers. (54) It seems that he says one thing, then later says or does something different.

Hillary Rodham Clinton V Donald J. Trump

Donald Trump

In 2017, Donald J Trump was sworn in to one of the most contentious presidencies in history. Trump's economic policies focused on cutting taxes, deregulation, and trade protectionism. (55) The deficit sharply increased while Trump was president. (56) Many supported his promise to put America first and bring back jobs from China. You may remember the MAGA campaign that stood for Make America Great Again.

Trump reversed a Consumer Financial Protection Bureau (CFPB) rule that helped consumers file class action suits against banks. The CFPB reduced enforcement of rules that protected consumers from predatory payday lenders. Trump reduced regulations against airlines, including a ruling that they disclose baggage fees. (57, 58) Trump also repealed part of the Dodd-Frank Act. Trump proposed changes to the food stamp program that would have led to millions losing their access and millions more having less. (59) We shouldn't wrap businesses in red tape. But we need to keep rules in place to protect consumers.

Trump sought to rebalance the trade deficit with China. He added tariffs to many products from the European Union, Canada, and Mexico. (60, 61) Trump pledged to withdraw from the Trans-Pacific Partnership. (62) We need to hold certain countries such as China accountable. But Trump's strategy appeared to be protectionist rather than targeted. He should have renegotiated the trade agreements with China and addressed the trade deficit. But he could have left the trade agreements with Canada and Europe in place. We should not raise tariffs on China to be protectionist. We should raise tariffs on China because they have done nothing to address the environment or workers' rights issues. If we give China a free pass, we are creating a loophole where companies can send jobs to China for cheap wages and thumb their noses at our environmental standards.

In 2017, Trump signed his tax bill. It lowered the corporate federal tax rate from 35% to 21%. (63) He cut the top individual tax rate from 39.6% to 37%. His tax bill doubled the standard deduction and repealed the individual mandate for health insurance under the Affordable Care Act. (64) Many people saw their tax bills decrease under Trump's tax bills. But it is estimated that 13.5% of middle-class families would have higher tax bills. (65) The wealthy already had enough tax cuts; they didn't need any more. Many economists estimated that the wealthy would benefit much more than the workers from the corporate tax cuts. (66) Trump should have done more to ensure that all middle-class families received tax relief and forgot about helping the wealthy.

It seems that Trump has already done everything he can do for the economy. A second term would just lead to more of the same. (67) He plans to pass a new tax bill. But we don't need any more tax cuts. We certainly don't need tax cuts for the wealthy. We don't need more deregulation. Trump's plans for trade seem to have more to do with retaliation against other nations than it does fair deals that would lead to good paying jobs. Trump's second presidency could be considered Trump's Revenge.

Hillary Rodham Clinton

Clinton called herself a progressive. (68) She seemed to have a strong and detailed economic plan. In 2001, she voted for a bankruptcy bill that would make it more difficult for borrowers to discharge their debts. (69) But in 2007, she introduced the Student Borrower Bill of Rights that would assist student borrowers to pay back their loans. (70) Clinton supported a constitutional amendment for campaign reform to limit the influence of the wealthy on campaigns. (71)

Clinton believed that the government did have a role to play in our economy. She said that there should be a 'healthy tension' between government and business. (72) In a 2014 speech, she decried trickle-down economics. (73) She condemned short-term capitalism and stated that capitalism "needs to be reinvented." She offered support for small businesses and the middle class. But she was not a supporter of the Nordic model of socialism. She stated that "We are Not Denmark. We are the United States" She felt that we should "reign in the excesses of capitalism' and "save capitalism from itself". Part of her plan would rescind tax relief and benefits for companies that move jobs overseas. She planned to provide incentives for profit sharing and focusing on employees, communities, and the environment. (74) A review of history will show that she was right and that her plan would have made improvements for many people. We need to hold business accountable. We need to have the government provide help as part of a social safety net. We need to do more to provide childcare for working families. She proposed expanding the childcare tax credits so that childcare expenses wouldn't exceed 10 percent of a household's income. (75) It is likely she would expand free trade. She admitted that as Senator, she voted for every property negotiated trade agreement. (76)

Clinton expressed support for more financial regulations for Wall Street. She would strengthen the Dodd-Frank regulations. (77) She supported a "New College Compact", expanding Obamacare, expanding early childhood education, increased spending on infrastructure, veterans, and research funding. (78) She pledged not to raise taxes on working- and middle-class families. (79) She proposed raising taxes on high-income earners and multinational corporations. (80) She would have added a 4% surcharge to taxpayers earning over $5 million per year, a 30% minimum tax rate on millionaires and increased taxes on long-term capital gains. (81) We should tax the wealthy more. Even billionaires such as Warren Buffet agree. (82)

During her 2016 campaign, Clinton proposed raising the federal minimum wage to $12 per hour. She also supported the Fight for $15 campaign. (83) As Senator, she voted to increase the minimum wage. (84) In 2014, she said "Don't let anyone tell you that raising the minimum wage will kill jobs – they always say that. I've been through this. My husband gave workers a raise in the 1990s. I voted to raise the minimum wage and guess what, millions of jobs were created or paid better, and more families were secure." (85) She described the current federal minimum wage of $7.25 as a starvation wage. (86)

President Joe Biden

In January 2021, Joe Biden took office as president. Biden is usually a strong supporter of unions. He signed an executive order to repeal schedule F that limited the collective bargaining power of federal unions. (87) He also promoted a $15 per hour minimum wage for federal workers and improved the employee discipline process. (88) During his campaign, he stated that he intended to fight laws that exist to deprive the unions of the support they need. (89) While Biden has received an 85% approval rating from the AFL-CIO, he did support legislation that would impose contracts that forced them to work without sick leave. He even used the Railway Labor Act to prevent them from striking. (90) In 2023, Biden was a strong supporter of the UAW during their most recent strike. (91)

In January 2021, Biden drafted the American Rescue Plan Act of 2021 in response to the pandemic of 2020. The plan included $1 trillion in direct aid, checks for $1,400 per person, and other programs to aid the country in recovery. (92) When the bill was signed into law in March, the provision to increase the minimum wage was excluded. (93) In April of the same year, he drafted the American Families Plan. This plan included spending roughly $1.8 trillion for programs for childcare, paid leave, community college, and healthcare. This bill did not pass. (94, 95) The second part of Biden's Build Back Better plan involved the American Jobs Plan. This plan intended to address the long-neglected infrastructure of our country. (96) Biden aimed to create millions of jobs, bolster labor unions, expand labor protections, and address climate change. (97) A budget of $621 billion was proposed for transportation infrastructure including highways, railways, public transportation, airports, and encouragement to adopt electric vehicles. There was a provision for infrastructure 'at home' that would provide $213 billion to build 2 million homes and improve public housing. The plan included $180 billion for research and development for clean energy. (98) The PRO Act was intended to Protect the Right to Organize. It would have overridden the state right-to-work laws. (99) Biden intended to raise the corporate tax rate from 21% to 28%. Before 2017, the corporate tax rate was 35%. He also wanted to restore the top individual tax rate to 39.6%. (100, 101) This bill didn't pass either. It could be that either the tax increases or the scope and cost of the plan caused it not to pass. In 2022, Biden was able to pass a much pared down version that was the Inflation Reduction Act. It would include a 15% minimum tax for companies showing a financial statement profit of more than $1 billion. (102) Biden seems to be on the right track with trying to raise taxes on the wealthy to invest in America. But his aggressive goals on reversing climate change may be limiting his ability to make lasting economic reform.

Biden opposes privatizing and means-testing for Social Security. He supports an expansion of Social Security that would increase payments to older Americans, set a minimum guaranteed benefit for those with sufficient credits, and increase monthly survivor benefits for widows and widowers. Biden would fund those improvements through tax increases on the highest income workers. (103)

As a Senator, Biden has tried to reduce trade barriers and set global trade standards. (104) He voted for NAFTA, Australia-U.S. Free Trade Agreement, and the Morocco-U.S. Free Trade Agreement. He voted against trade agreements with Singapore, Chile, Oman, and Central America because their labor and environmental protections were insufficient. (105) He voted for the trade agreements with China in 1998 and 2000 as well as the Trans-Pacific Partnership. (106) Biden has been critical of Chinese trade tactics, and he believes the U.S. should govern trade rather than China. He states that workers, the environment, and middle-class wages should be protected. (107) In March 2021, the U.S. stated that they would not lift tariffs on Chinese imports in the near future. Biden and U.S. Secretary of Commerce Gina Raimondo plan to aggressively enforce trade rules to combat China's unfair practices. (108, 109) We need to hold China accountable and make lowering the tariffs dependent on wage and environmental reform in China. If wages in China are like ours, there will not be such an incentive to send jobs over there.

When President Biden campaigned in 2020, he expressed his support for raising the federal minimum wage to $15 per hour. He attempted to add this provision as part of his stimulus plan. But after the proposal was shot down in March of 2021, he hasn't tried to raise the minimum wage since. He has suggested that the state governors raise their minimum wage. Many states do have minimum wages that are higher than the federal rate. Currently, the Raise the Wage Act of 2023 is seeking to raise the minimum wage to $17 per hour. (17) He is quoted as saying "No one should work 40 hours a week and be living in poverty." He's right. We need to make this happen.

President Biden has issued an order that 50 percent of vehicles sold in 2030 should be electric vehicles. Plugin hybrids are included in the 50 percent, but we seem to be pushing fully electric vehicles. (110) This is an example of government overreach. The people are being pushed to adopt a technology that isn't mature enough to meet their needs. There are three problems with our quest to be gas free.

First, batteries take their toll on the environment too. There is plenty of pollution and energy needed to mine the materials and manufacture the batteries. Mining produces its own share of pollution. If we were to switch to EVs, we would reduce our dependence on foreign oil. But who would provide our batteries? If we could make these in America, that would be one reason to make the switch.

The second issue with converting to electric vehicles is that we have an entire infrastructure dedicated to gasoline vehicles. Adding enough charging stations for the new electric vehicles would be a massive undertaking. Who would pay for this switch?

The third issue has to do with the use and perception of these new vehicles. Many must be convinced that the electric vehicles will meet their needs. (111) Gas is expensive and finite, but it is convenient. When I fill my gas tank, I can get a range of over 400 miles before I must fill up again. Once I run out of gas, it takes about 5 minutes to fill up the tank and be on my way.   If I forget to get gas, I can just stop by a gas station for 5 minutes. In the worst-case scenario, I would have to fill up a gas can and then drive to a gas station. What happens with electric vehicles? How long does it take to charge at home? My electric lawn equipment takes about an hour. When I used gas, I could fill the tank instantly.   Now, I must plan ahead and make sure my equipment is charged before I use it. How long does it take to charge an electric car at a charging station?   How expensive is it? I have also read that electric vehicles have different fuel ranges depending on the temperature.   It seems that there are too many unknowns to fully commit to using an electric vehicle. These headaches are likely to cause us problems in the future.

The U.S. economy was hit by massive inflation in 2022. There were several causes for the inflation. The pandemic caused massive supply chain disruptions that helped to drive up the prices. Pent up demand contributed to the rise in prices. Wage increases were needed to encourage workers to take jobs due to the extra demands of the pandemic. Biden's stimulus package contributed too. Add to that the political problems with Russia and Israel and you have a perfect storm for inflation. Biden's energy policy also contributed to the high inflation. The low interest rates caused housing prices to spiral out of control once the pandemic eased. The stimulus packages, low interest rates, and wage increases were all necessary measures to keep the economy on track due to the pandemic. The supply and demand, and foreign conflicts can't be helped. The only action we could take was to change our energy policy to lower gas prices. While inflation reached a peak of 9.1% in

June 2022, it has eased to a moderate rate of 3.2% as of the end of 2023. (112, 113, 114, 115)

The Other Candidates

Two of the candidates running for president have already had a turn. But it looks like we are going to have a rematch of the 2020 election. Trump would cut taxes for the wealthy, deregulate business, and continue the tariffs against China. He is likely to raise tariffs against other countries. The wealthy don't need any more tax cuts or deregulation. We should have tariffs against China because they are not committed to reforms regarding wages or the environment. We should use tariffs as a tool to encourage positive change. But we shouldn't raise tariffs just to create barriers and hamper free trade.

President Biden still has some work to do. We need to raise the minimum wage. He has at least a year left to make it happen. According to his history, he is likely to help unions, tax the wealthy, build infrastructure, expand social security, and continue to push the electric vehicle agenda. He may still hold China accountable. It would be best if President Biden could reassure us of his commitment to protect workers, tax the wealthy, and rebuild our infrastructure. Even a pared down infrastructure plan is better than nothing. He should reassure us of his commitment to hold China accountable. China has not honored the terms of the agreement that gave them favorable trading status. After reviewing the charts and data for 2000 to present, the same trends continue. While the GDP, Dow Jones, and productivity soar, the wealth of the

1% and our costs of living are still outpacing our gains in wages.

There were two other Democratic candidates running for president in 2024. They were Dean Phillips and Marianne Williamson. These candidates are no longer running for president.

Dean Phillips is a U.S. representative from Minnesota. He planned to focus on bringing down the cost of living by being pro-worker and pro-business, addressing mental health and drug issues, investing in young people, and pursuing term limits, campaign finance reform, and bipartisan presidential Cabinets. (116) We need campaign reform to limit the influence of the wealthy on politics. But I could not find more detail about Phillips' plan for the economy.

Marianne Williamson was a presidential primary candidate in 2020. Her focus was on economic issues, universal healthcare, tuition-free higher education, paid parental leave and a minimum wage increase. Her agenda included fundamental economic reform. (117) Williamson has published an economic bill of rights that has some good ideas. These would include the right to healthcare, education, housing, and a fair wage. (118)

There were many Republican presidential candidates for 2024. Previous alternate candidates included Ryan Binkley, Doug Burgum, Chris Christie, Ron DeSantis, Nikki Haley, Asa Hutchinson, and Vivek Ramaswamy.

Ryan Binkley is a businessman and pastor. His campaign focused on reducing the national debt by lowering federal spending, reducing healthcare costs, increasing border security, streamlining the process for legal immigration, and increasing community involvement in education. Lowering the national debt is important, but it is not the highest priority. I could not find a strong economic plan for Ryan Binkley. (119)

Doug Burgum has been the governor of North Dakota since 2016. He planned to focus on energy production, the economy, and national security. He would cut taxes, reduce inflation, and increase domestic energy production. I could not find whether those tax cuts would go to the middle class or the wealthy. The wealthy certainly don't need any more help. (120)

Christopher Christie was the governor of New Jersey for two terms. He seems to have a mixed record on the economy. He stated that he was in favor of raising the minimum wage but vetoed a constitutional amendment to raise the wage in New Jersey. It should not take a constitutional amendment to raise the minimum wage. This is something that every worker deserves. (121)

Ron DeSantis is currently the governor of Florida. He promised to reduce government spending and inflation. He would increase security for the U.S.-Mexico border, support law enforcement, and increase domestic energy production. He planned to lower individual tax rates, slash regulations, and overhaul the tax system to encourage corporations to invest in the U.S. long term. He would have added a work requirement to social safety net programs. His plans involved challenging China on its trade imbalance. (122, 123) Where would he cut spending? Who would benefit most from the tax cuts? How would he have planned to increase domestic energy production? His campaign seemed to be more about combating 'wokeness' than protecting workers.

Nikki Haley was the U.N. Ambassador in the Trump administration. She would have focused on foreign policy, economic, and immigration issues. Before serving as U.N.

Ambassador, Haley was the governor of South Carolina from 2011 to 2017. She planned to cut middle class taxes, tackle inflation, and reduce federal spending. Her Freedom Plan would eliminate federal gas taxes and reduce income taxes. Small-business tax relief would become permanent. Middle class tax cuts would help the general public. We do need to curb spending and help small businesses. But we also need to raise the minimum wage and hold big business accountable. Haley was the last Republican candidate to cede to Donald Trump. (124, 125)

Asa Hutchinson was the governor of Arkansas from 2015 to 2023. His priorities would involve reducing government spending, increasing security at the U.S.-Mexico border, and supporting law enforcement. When researching his campaign, I found more criticisms of Bidenomics than concrete plans to protect workers. (126)

Vivek Ramaswamy is an entrepreneur, political commentator, and author. He planned to reduce the size of the federal government, support freedom of speech, oppose environmental, social, and corporate governance, oppose China, and oppose affirmative action. (127) But I don't see a plan to help workers.

If you can't find a candidate that you like in the Democratic or Republican party, perhaps you might like the independent or third-party candidates. These include Cornel West (Independent), Jill Stein (Green Party), Chase Oliver (Libertarian Party) and Robert F. Kennedy Jr. who is running as an independent candidate after withdrawing from the Democratic primary.

Cornel West is an academic and an activist. West has described himself as a 'non-Marxist socialist'. He formerly sought to run under the Green Party. I believe that socialism wouldn't be a good fit for America. (128)

Jill Stein is a physician, organizer, and environmental-health advocate. She is running for president with the Green Party. Stein's platform focuses on combating climate change and a Green New Deal. She supports the Economic Bill of Rights that would guarantee a living wage, housing, food, health care and education. (129, 130)

Chase Oliver is running for President for the Libertarian Party. One of the core tenets of Libertarianism is laissez-faire capitalism and government non-interference. (131) We need the government to regulate capitalism so that it won't continue to be the dog-eat-dog bloodbath that we have now.

Robert Kennedy Jr. is an author and lawyer for environmental and healthcare-related law. He is the son of Robert F. Kennedy and nephew of John F. Kennedy. Kennedy plans to bring back jobs, help unions, raise the minimum wage, rein in healthcare costs, and control immigration. He pledges to support small businesses. (132,133) Kennedy seems to have a great plan for protecting workers' rights. But he doesn't have political experience.

Kamala Harris

If President Biden is reelected, Vice President Kamala Harris will become president if Biden becomes unable to fulfill his duties. Harris has said that she is not a socialist, but more needs to be done to ensure equal opportunities for working people. (134) In 2020, Harris introduced the Price Gouging Prevention act that would enforce a ban on excessive price increases amid national emergencies such as the Pandemic. Ten percent would be considered price gouging. (135) Harris stated she would not have voted for NAFTA because "we can do a better job to protect American workers". (136) In 2017, she announced that she would co-sponsor Bernie Sanders' Medicare for All bill that would support single-payer healthcare. (137) She opposed the Tax Cuts and Jobs Act of 2017 and has called for a repeal of the bill's tax cuts for wealthy Americans. (138) She would also support increasing taxes on corporations. (139) Harris has also committed to raising the minimum wage to $15 per hour. (140) But after three years, the federal minimum wage is still at $7.25 per hour. There is currently the Raise the Wage Act circulating in Congress that needs to pass.

We will not be able to find the perfect candidate who agrees with us completely. But we should be able to demand certain things such as a minimum wage increase. Once a candidate is elected, we can always make requests. In the next chapters, I will explore what we need to do and how we can motivate our politicians to give us what we need.

CHAPTER EIGHT

REFORM! WHAT WE NEED TO DO FOR CHANGE

REFORM! WHAT WE NEED TO DO FOR CHANGE

Now that we have reviewed history, what should we do to make lasting change? We need a concentrated list of demands on our leaders. We will explore different solutions.

Raise The Minimum Wage

Before we enacted the Minimum Wage in 1938, workers were paid less than a quarter an hour. Entire families would live in dirty one-room apartments in the city. (1,2,3) The intent of the minimum wage law was to pay workers enough to support themselves and their families. Adam Smith commented that a worker must be paid enough to support a family, or else the workers will die out in a generation. (Smith, page 57) Without a mandated floor for wages, employers would pay wages that left families in poverty. The last time we raised the minimum wage was 15 years ago when Obama raised the limit to $7.25 per hour in 2009. Before this, the minimum wage was raised at least once a decade. Sometimes it was increased once a year. (4) The minimum wage must be raised regularly because of inflation. It is estimated that the current minimum wage is not sufficient to cover the costs of living. Even the middle class is struggling to pay the bills. (5) If we are serious about having a minimum wage, we should tie pay to increase with the rate of inflation. Otherwise, the concept of a minimum wage becomes meaningless.

Many would argue that raising the minimum wage would cause higher inflation. They might argue that a minimum wage shuts out those willing to work for a lower wage. Some worry that raising the wage will cause wage-push inflation that will force corporations to raise prices to maintain their bottom line. Perhaps raising wages would cause small businesses to be less competitive. But there is not a lot of empirical data to support the wage-push inflation concern. In 2016, the W.E. Upjohn Institute for Employment Research reviewed the effect on prices of minimum wage increases from 1978 to 2015. They found that prices grew by 0.36 percent for every 10 percent increase in the minimum wage. Those increases happened in the few months following the increase, but not much after. Raising the minimum wage did not cause runaway inflation. (6) There are several reasons that raising the federal minimum wage may not cause runaway inflation. The current push for $17 per hour reflects a demand that is already being made. Much progress was made during the Great Resignation. The Great Resignation was a time when many determined that their current pay and jobs weren't working for them. So, they left their old jobs and demanded more pay. (7) It is not that people don't want to work anymore. They just don't want to struggle with several jobs that expose them to the public for poor wages. Many have already managed to make more than the minimum wage. Some fast-food restaurants offer to pay $11 to $14 per hour. Some states have a minimum wage that is higher than $7.25 per hour. But raising the federal minimum wage would protect everyone to ensure they can make a living wage. Part of the inflation we experienced may have come from the higher pay that workers have already received. But the economy has absorbed these higher wages and inflation has cooled. (8) While payroll makes up a large percentage of a company's expenses, wages aren't the only expenses that companies pay. Companies pay rent, costs to produce goods, advertising, building costs, and utilities. A one percent increase in wages does not translate into a one percent increase in all costs. Raising the minimum wage does not lead to a raise for everyone. You may receive more pay if you make a wage near the minimum. But if you make double the new minimum wage, you probably wouldn't receive a raise once the minimum wage is increased. Raising the minimum wage from $7.25 an hour to $17 an hour may sound drastic, but some have already received increases. Raising the federal minimum wage would just ensure that everyone is protected. We need to demand that our politicians make the new wage a reality so that we can protect all workers. If the federal government doesn't raise the minimum wage, we can always demand that our state step up to the plate. At least 30 states already have a minimum wage above the federal rate. (9)

In 2022, the European Union voted to approve a new minimum wage directive. This directive instructs those European countries with a minimum wage to reanalyze their wages to ensure that the minimum wage will be enough to pay for household expenses. Some European countries have a culture that provides strong collective bargaining that keeps wages fair. general, Europe now does a better job of protecting workers. (10, 11) In France, people work 35 hours a week instead of 40. In the Netherlands, the minimum wage is adjusted twice a year, not once every 15 years. Other countries analyze it once a year. (12) European workers take more breaks and work less hours. American's often brag about how many hours they work and how little they sleep. But who benefits from this extreme dedication? (13)

The Job Market

Looking for a job these days is a nightmare. The market is extremely competitive, and the employers are extremely stingy. When I updated my resume on the Internet, I had at least ten calls a day. But they all wanted to pay less than what I was currently making. California and Colorado are taking a step in the right direction by mandating that employers place a salary range in their job postings. (14) Nothing is worse than jumping through so many hoops just to find that you are being offered a job paying less money than you already make. A few years after I graduated from college, I interviewed for an accounting job at a dealership. At the end of the interview, I was offered $5.50 per hour. A couple years before, I was paid $5.25 per hour to clean toilets at McDonalds. While the wage posting requirements are an important step, we may have more work to do. Recently, I had two interviews for an accounting position that posted a salary of $85,000 to $116,000. I didn't get the job. When I asked for the middle at $100,000/year, they told me it was a good thing I didn't ask for $116,000. They had no intention of paying $116,000. Then why did they put that on the job posting? I believe that they were stringing me along. They probably had no intention of paying $100,000 either. Someone else probably offered to work for $85,000 and they now have the job. The games companies play.

Has anyone else sent hundreds or thousands of resumes on the Internet only to hear NOTHING from any of the companies? My favorite is when they ask you to send a resume, then they require you to enter the exact same information again on their forms. And when you do, you waste this time to go into a file. Talk about no respect for your time. Many companies require that you set up an account with a password. Some job postings are even scams. With some of the names of these sites, it becomes hard to tell what is real and what is a scam. Another favorite is when you try to fill out an application only to have it repeatedly error out. I have read that some jobs are posted for reasons other than filling active roles. Companies may post job openings to 'show that they are growing' or to placate their current employees with the promise of help that will never come. Unfortunately, we can't always outlaw bad behavior or inefficiency. We may not even be able to force bosses to treat employees with respect. But we can limit how businesses treat their employees. We can also provide government-based jobs that will be made to treat employees with the respect and fairness that they deserve.

In Europe, it is much more difficult to terminate an employee. Often, there is a contract that details the time each party must notify the other that they wish to terminate. In Spain, companies are required to have a 'valid reason' to terminate an employee. (15) Severance packages in some countries are required to pay one month of pay for every year the employee has worked. (16) We can consider doing that in the U.S. But we may have difficulties employing these laws in the United States. Companies already drag their feet when it comes to hiring.

We need to do something to help those who become displaced by job losses. Imagine this. You set up your entire life around the fact that you have a good paying job. You show up and work very hard. As far as you know, you will have this job until you retire. This job even becomes part of who you are. Then one day, you are told that your services are no longer needed. The entire bedrock of your financial existence has been taken away. Your entire financial future comes crashing down. How will you feed the kids? How will you pay for the house? Will you lose the house? Will you ever find a job that pays as well as the last job? With massive layoffs, many workers end up making less at their next job. The WARN act was passed in 1988 to help those who may become the victim of a mass layoff. It states that companies who have more than 100 employees must provide 60 days' notice if they intend to terminate more than 50 people at a single site. Employers are required to provide job-training and transition programs for these employees. But are these programs enough? (17) I remember watching Roger & Me. Ronald Reagan, Pat Boone, and Anita Bryant assured everyone that it would all work out. It didn't. (18) We need to do a better job by making job placement programs to help families displaced by massive layoffs. Perhaps we should even make the companics pay for these programs. Until now, we just leave workers to fend for themselves. I have always found the job-hunting process to be a sick and sadistic game of musical chairs.

Raise Taxes on the Wealthy

The wealthy have had enough tax breaks. Reagan lowered the top individual tax rate from 70% to 50%. (19,22) George W. Bush lowered the top individual tax rate from 39.6% to 35%. (20,22) Then Trump lowered the top individual tax rate from 39.6% to 37%. (21) We need to raise taxes on the wealthy. Research suggests that the optimal point on the Laffer Curve would be to raise the top individual rate to 60%. (23) We could then use this money to reduce the deficit or create jobs through government projects that would benefit the people.   Trickle-down economics suggests that if you let the wealthy keep more of their money, they will reinvest the money in the U.S. to create more jobs. This has not been working. If we raise taxes to pay for government provided jobs, we can ensure that the money will be invested in the U.S. Bush lowered the top capital gains rate from 8% to 5%. It was later raised to a maximum of 15%. (24,25) Many use capital gains receipts to fund their retirement. So, we should have a tiered tax system for capital gains. Those who have less than $1 million in capital gains can have the reduced rates while capital gains over $1 million can be taxed at a higher rate.

Reagan lowered the corporate tax rate from 48% to 34%. (26) Then Trump lowered the corporate tax rate again to 21%. (27) We gave corporations tax cuts with the expectation that they would provide jobs for American workers. That has not happened. I propose that we raise the corporate tax rates until we can maximize the tax revenues. Then we can use that money to make government jobs and/or reduce the federal deficit. You may believe that we should lower taxes as much as possible. I would not feel bad for the wealthy. Those in charge certainly don't feel bad for you. Many of the wealthy look down on people because they "made poor choices". They think they are better than us because they have more money. I wouldn't worry about defending the tax cuts for the wealthy. They won't share any of their money with you. Milton Friedman wrote that businesses should concern themselves only with maximizing the shareholders wealth. (Friedman, p 133) Business should not be concerned with fairness or the public good. As voters, we should vote for what is in our best interest. History has shown that the public does better with financial regulations and taxing the wealthy. I am not concerned with equality of wages or sharing the wealth. I am saying that we should raise taxes on the wealthy to spend that money for the common good. We should regulate business to be sure that workers are paid their fair share. We do this because we believe that it will create the greatest good for the greatest number for voters. We should feel no guilt for voting for a society that benefits the most people even if it is at the expense of the wealthy. The wealthy and their business use most of the resources, so they should pay for them. I want to propose a new idea about policy. John Stuart Mill wrote that the principle aim of any action should be that which makes the most people happy or eases the pain of the most people. (28) Marginal utility would suggest that an additional dollar is more valuable if you have fewer dollars. As you get more dollars, each extra dollar provides a diminishing marginal utility. So, if we take money from the rich, they are less likely to miss it than if it is taken from the poor. If we let the poor keep an extra dollar, it will mean more to them. This is the concept behind progressive taxes. (29)

The wealthy often pay less than the middle class. (30) They are getting a free ride. The 1% get all the rewards while we pay all the costs and accept all the risks. Just look at the Great Recession. The Wall Street Bankers received all the rewards, and we were stuck with the bailout bill because they were 'too big to fail'. (31) The wealthy have all the money, and we are left to drive on crumbling roads. Corporations should pay more taxes because they use more resources. For example, businesses cause more wear on our roads because they drive their trucks to sell their goods. We only drive our cars.

Previously, I proposed that we raise the federal tax rates. I propose this for the greater good and not just to punish the wealthy. I would suggest that the states keep their taxes the same. States tend to have simpler tax codes that aren't as progressive. The federal government would be most able to manage the taxing and spending of the wealthy. But the federal government isn't the only entity that should consider raising taxes. I propose that every state, county, city that has property taxes enact a homestead exemption. This exemption would allow primary residences to be taxed at a lower rate. Commercial real estate would be levied separately. The homestead exemption would not apply to vacation homes and investment properties. The lower taxes would help to make primary homes more affordable. It's no secret that investors are driving up the prices of homes. I propose that if a person has enough money for a second home or investment property, then they have enough money to pay more taxes for those properties. Non-homestead taxes should produce a downward pressure on prices of residential real estate.

While I advocate for raising taxes on businesses and the wealthy, this is only for those that can afford to pay the taxes. Taxes should only be raised on profits. There are some taxes and fees that businesses pay just to operate. Not every business is raking in the dough. If a small business is struggling to be profitable, it is our duty to lighten their tax load. We should also keep taxes low on the working class. In some cases, we even offer Earned Income Credits. If a person has a family and they don't reach a certain threshold, they will receive money from the federal government in the form of a tax credit. Even if the tax credit is greater than their expected tax, they get the full value of the credit in their refund. (32) As a society, we should want all businesses to succeed. But it is better for society if profitable businesses pay their fair share. There are some tax laws that help small businesses. Businesses can carry forward losses for 20 years or carry back losses for up to five years. The time limits change based on the changes in tax laws. Carry back losses have ranged from zero to five years depending on the goals of the current administration. (33) This means that if a business has a profitable year preceded by years of losses, that business can apply the previous losses against its current tax bill. We just need to be sure that those businesses don't run into problems with the Alternative Minimum Tax. Businesses who need help should be able to lower their tax bill without barriers. (34) When we tax the wealthy and mega corporations, we are taxing after profits and living expenses. Corporate taxes only affect profitable businesses. If a business is struggling, they would only have to pay for payroll taxes.

Many countries in Europe tax corporate profits at 20-30%. (35) While corporate tax rates are at or below the average rate in Europe, we need to consider financing the needs of our country. Our taxes should reflect what we need here. If we can finance the needs of our society with a lower corporate tax rate, then we shouldn't artificially raise the rates. We want to compete, but we don't want to leave people to starve.

While we want to adequately fund our society, we don't want to put undue burden on our businesses. We want the businesses to pay their fair share, but we want them to succeed. If the businesses succeed, we can tax them. We want to reduce any taxes or fees that prevent a company from being profitable. But we want to tax the profit. We want to reduce the burden of taxation as well. In Canada, they impose a Value Added Tax or VAT. (36) When a business buys something, they pay a tax to the seller who then pays Canada. The business gets a refund for the tax they paid until they reach the consumer. There are a lot of ins and outs, and it is very complicated. At each stage, the businesses pay taxes then seek refunds. Meanwhile, the government makes interest on the money they are holding. In the US, each reseller is exempt from taxes until they sell to the retail customer. The retail customer pays the same amount either way. With the American method of wholesaling, the businesses have a lot less paperwork and administrative burden.

Social Security

Our Social Security program is projected to go bankrupt before 2040. (37) During the golden era of unions, many workers had pensions. But now, most workers are unprepared for retirement because the responsibility has been shifted on to them. (38, 39) We need to strengthen our commitment to social security. We need to shore up our social security by taxing the wealthy more. We have already raised the limit that is taxed for social security and Medicare. But we may want to consider adding taxes for employers so that Social Security will be able to fulfill its role. If enough people want to raise Social Security taxes, we can make it happen. We will have to carefully balance the budget. If we raise taxes on the wealthy, we should use some to increase Social Security and the rest to lower the deficit so that we can spend less on interest. We need to be sure that our programs are well funded. But fiscal policy is a balancing act. We also need to work on reducing our deficit. In 2022, interest payments on the national debt reached $475 billion. It's estimated that in 10 years, interest costs will exceed spending on programs such as Medicaid and defense. (40) Our large deficit puts the financial future of our country at risk.

We are over 40 years into our experiment with personal 401k retirement accounts and that system has failed us miserably! There are several reasons why the 401k was such a terrible idea. When we switched from pensions to 401k accounts, we received a pay cut. With pensions, the company would set aside the needed funds for our retirement. Now, we must set aside at least 5% of our pay for our own retirement. With pensions, we had experts who would manage the company pension accounts. Now, we are left to fend for ourselves. Most of us are not skilled with investments. It's not our fault. The benefit of combining assets into a pool is that the retirement fund can afford to get the best people who do have investment expertise. Many of us are unable or unqualified to make the choices needed to succeed in navigating the maze to a comfortable retirement. Should we be surprised? Is it right that we leave retirement to individuals, and then fault them if they don't' make all the right choices? The last reason we need pooled investments has to do with risk management. With a combined fund such as pensions and social security, you can predict how many people will live to certain ages. It is a game of statistics. As you gain a bigger pool, you can more easily predict how that sample size will act as a whole. But with a single person, there is no way to predict what will happen. With a large pool, you can accurately determine how much you need to provide for retirement funds. With single retirement accounts, we all must save enough money so that we can afford to live until we are 90. This places a much heavier burden on us than it does a company. We all must invest so much more. Many will save enough to last until they are 90 only to die much sooner. Some won't be able to save that much and will have a long but poor life.

This is why it is important that we expand and protect our social security system.

Filing Taxes

We have an odd situation here in the United States. Everyone who pays you reports what they paid to the Internal Revenue Service shortly after the year ends. But the IRS doesn't tell you what they reported. They rely on you to put together all the different pieces of information through the mail, then struggle to figure out what you owe. You must pull all the pieces together and report what you made. With electronic information exchange, the IRS knows what you made before you do! In countries such as Denmark, Sweden, Spain, the United Kingdom, they have Ready Return. The revenue agencies let you see what others have reported. They estimate your taxes and refunds, then you just verify that the information is correct. (41,42) Once we file our taxes here in the United States, we better make sure we don't miss anything. Because if we do, the IRS will use the information they have to charge us interest and penalties for any mistakes we make. It's even worse now that some payers don't mail their tax reports. Some banks require you to download these forms from your account. What if you forget about an account or job? Most of us are not tax experts. Filing taxes has a definite cost in terms of time and money. Many who are poor feel they can't afford to file. At worst, they are charged penalties and interest because they can't afford to pay to have their taxes filed. If you can't afford to have an expert file your taxes, you may miss out on refunds and tax credits you can receive. But many leave money on the table because they can't afford to pay to file taxes. Others pay ridiculous 'interest' to have tax preparers give them loans for a faster refund. This results in a 'tax' on the poor. In Europe, people don't have these problems. Their governments are more transparent. We can do better than playing these games.

Healthcare

We are one of the few industrialized countries in the world that does not have universal healthcare. Yet the United States also tends to have the worst health outcomes compared to other industrialized countries. (43) Every year, millions are financially ruined when they have expensive medical bills they can't afford. (44) We need to do something to help those who can't afford health care coverage. Solutions include expanding Medicaid or offering a Nation-Wide catastrophic coverage. Some states have already expanded Medicaid to include families whose income is below 133% of the poverty level. We should demand that every state expand their Medicaid to include struggling families. (45) We can't afford a Cadillac style of coverage for everyone. But can we have a limited plan that would keep people from being ruined by an unforeseen healthcare emergency? The concept of insurance is for everyone to pool their money together to help those in the pool who face calamity. Any one of us can face a medical emergency. It may be in our best interest to be sure that everyone is covered. An example would be someone losing their job, then having a major auto accident that needs surgery. This policy should be one that can be used for anyone whose medical bills reach a certain amount in a year. There would not be a mandatory enrollment because all citizens would be automatically eligible if they don't have employer sponsored insurance or Medicare. This would better cover people who don't have income. The Obamacare mandate did not have any penalties for those who had no income to file for taxes. Since this plan would be basic coverage for those who can't afford it, it should leave the employer-based plans to be run by the market. If a person has the money, they should be able to buy any plan they can afford. The purpose of the government plan is to cover medical costs for the poor, and not to run all medical insurance. The American people do not want to have the government run all health care reimbursement because we value freedom of choice. The market does fine when people have money. We only need the government to help those who can't afford insurance.

While we need to help those who need it, we need to be careful that we don't limit the options for our healthcare. Many European countries have a universal healthcare system. The government just pays for everyone regardless of their income level. But there are some issues with Universal Healthcare. Access can be sporadic. There is a concern that there aren't enough doctors to treat everyone and that there will be long wait times and long-distance travel to receive certain medical procedures. Europe is also facing many challenges due to its aging population and the COVID crisis. (46) Universal Healthcare would not be wanted by many Americans because of these issues and the American preference for choice.

Education

Adam Smith wrote that skilled labor is the most valuable commodity that a nation can have. (Smith, page 4) If that is true, then why do we leave it up to individuals to get an education for their livelihood? Some countries in Europe fully fund the education for their children through college.

Other countries charge nominal fees or low tuition. (47) But we leave our children to shoulder massive debt at the start of their careers. (48) Then we pay recent grads as little as possible. (49) We wonder why we are having a crisis amongst our young people. Why don't we tax the wealthy more to pay for the education of their workers? The wealthy will be the ones who benefit most from educated workers. We can't say that we don't believe in using taxes for education. We already tax property owners to pay for education through high school. We have paid for higher education for our children in the past. (50,51, 52) But we decided to saddle our children with massive debt in the eighties. Apparently, Reagan didn't want there to be too many educated workers asking too many questions. Richard Nixon started Sallie Mae in 1972. He intended to make it easier to invest in college loans. It is believed that by making an easy market to finance education, he helped to cause the college costs to grow. Why not charge more if you can get students to borrow more? (48)

While the government, and by extension the people, should pay for higher education, there should be a few strings attached. When we send a child to college, we are making an investment. The degree should go to something that will provide gainful employment. We want to educate our children to be able to make a living and produce for the good of our society. If you are just curious and like to read, you can read all you like for free at the library. Children who want to apply for college should put in the work to ensure that they will do well in college. College applicants should have good grades in high school or good grades from a community school that can be transferred. When our society invests in a child, we want to be sure that the child will succeed. It is wasteful to pay for a child to drop out and just receive 'the college experience'. We may need to consider offering free education for public universities. The plan would be to limit costs.

We need to reconsider our model for education and jobs in this country. Many years ago, most skilled workers had small businesses. People would learn a trade that they used to support their families for their entire career. Now, we work for a piece of paper so that someone else will hire us and pay our salaries. We are educated so that we can be workers in someone else's business. We get our education and then go begging for jobs so that we can make a living. Many business owners remark that they can't hire someone who takes the business as seriously as the owner. Adam Smith wrote that there is no incentive like building your own fortune. If we can move society towards a more entrepreneurial mindset, we will have businesses that provide more opportunity and meaning for those who run them. We don't teach our children to be entrepreneurs. We teach them to be cogs in the system. When the system breaks down, people lose their jobs and maybe even their homes. When there is a recession, many lose their jobs. These people have no alternative but to hope for a handout from the government. But if we trained people to be able to make their own opportunities, then those people would be better suited to handle downturns in the economy. Having many more small business owners would also help to provide more equality in our economic system. It has been a long time since I have attended high school. So, I have no idea what they teach. My impression is that we don't teach people the skills they need to succeed or survive. We should teach our high school students how to run a business. We need to teach skills to survive such as financial literacy. It doesn't matter if they run a store, design, consult, or handle plumbing. Each of these professions require some business knowledge to keep the cash flowing. We need to update our education system so that people can make their own jobs. We need to teach our kids how to survive and succeed. Then our children wouldn't be beholden to 'the man'. We would also need to pass small business friendly legislation and bankruptcy laws that would allow a clean slate for failures.

There is a debate as to whether the federal government should forgive student loans. There never should have been loans to forgive. Society benefits from educating our children. Educated people are our greatest asset. Other countries provide free or low-cost education to their citizens. If a college graduate is saddled with debt, then they may not be able to get the credit needed to start a business or buy a home. This represents a tax on the economy from less business activity and fewer home sales.

How did higher education become so expensive?!

It's well established that since the federal and state governments have cut support for higher education, the students are left to shoulder the cost of education on their own. Public universities have been raising tuition prices more than private universities. Public institutions have raised their tuition by 27% while public institutions have raised their tuition by 16%. (53) Universities have no requirement to be transparent with their pricing or expenses. There is no legal limit to how much schools can charge. Many college cost increases have come from expanded services and 'administrative expenses'.

A college education is in demand because it is considered a 'golden ticket'. Since there is so much demand

and ready financing, colleges can charge as much as they want because the students can just finance the costs. This debt then follows students through much of their lives. (54, 55, 56)

I have a few thoughts on how to contain college costs. I recommend in-state schools to out of state schools. The schools in the state will charge a lower tuition. Some colleges require students to live in dorms the first few years. If colleges were made to ease those rules, some students could attend college and live at home. I have often wondered why there were so many elective courses required. These courses do not contribute to a career. The standard argument is that electives help a student pursue fields of interest to be a well-rounded person. But I wonder if it is worth the cost. I don't see how being well-rounded would help pay off a mountain of debt. New graduates certainly don't get the pay for being well-rounded. When making career choices, I like to ask if the cost will produce a good payoff.

The government should provide more support for higher education. This is especially true for public universities. Public organizations should be audited to ensure that the colleges are being run effectively.

Infrastructure

It is no secret that our public infrastructure is crumbling. Our roads, bridges, and public transportation are far beyond their expected lives. (57) But we still struggle to pass legislation to fix these issues. We need a strong infrastructure bill. Perhaps we would want a federal department of roads that would use the tax money to keep our infrastructure in repair. We can make good paying government jobs that are designed to provide stable employment. The government can act as a standard bearer for the workforce. For roads that belong to the state or county, the federal government could finance the repair of those roads. There could even be a stipulation that workers be paid a certain wage for the state to qualify for the grants.

We could use government funded Research & Development. We need to develop a good system for public transportation and home-grown green energy. There is still much to be done to be sure that the new Electric Vehicle technology is reliable. Biden wants to force us to abandon Internal Combustion Engines in favor of Electric Vehicles. I once heard that an electric vehicle can be 'fast charged' from 20% to 80% in 26 minutes. Some Tesla cars can be charged in as little as fifteen minutes. This assumes you have the highest capacity fast chargers. But lower capacity chargers will take much longer. But you shouldn't let the battery go below 20% and you shouldn't fill the battery higher than 80% of capacity. (84) Does that mean you only get to use 60% of the capacity of the battery? We get to use the entire capacity of our gas tank. The car runs the same on almost empty as it does when it is topped off. It's just a matter of how many miles the car will take you. I once timed how long it would take to fill a tank from empty. It was less than five minutes. I have this picture of long lines and backups because it takes so long to charge the batteries. I have also read that electric trucks lose towing capacity in the cold. (59) We are over committed. We need a government program to research ways to provide the portability and flexibility of ICE engines. Why must we rush to use electric vehicles? I currently own a hybrid vehicle and it works great. We need to ensure that we can have home-grown green technology to end our dependence on foreign oil. We need to be sure that we have built enough infrastructure to power these electric vehicles before we commit.

Government Regulation

Not all regulation is bad. We need regulation for Wall Street Bankers so that they don't take unnecessary risks with our money. During the Great Recession, the banks raked in all the money while we paid the price in lost jobs and deficit spending to bail the banks out. (60) We need regulations to ensure that workers are being paid fairly. But we need to carefully consider why we are making regulations. We need regulations to counter crises such as the Great Recession and the Great Depression. But we need to limit regulations because they place a constraint on businesses. Our goal should be to ensure that business is ethical, not to run companies out of business.

Many of our workers are worried about good jobs going to Mexico or China. (61) It started with NAFTA. (62) Then it accelerated with China. (63) Companies can pay workers far less in these countries with no regard to the environment. Then they can sell goods in the U.S. for far cheaper. We need to hold these countries and companies accountable. There is no reason we should lower tariffs for countries that aren't committed to fair pay and a clean environment. We should also place extra taxes on companies who use labor from these countries. The workers in China and Mexico are being exploited. We can use our trade policies to further the agenda for change. It is safe to have free trade with Canada and Europe. I haven't heard of many concerns of jobs being shipped to Europe.

Over one hundred years ago, Theodore Roosevelt busted many trusts and monopolies. (64) These actions were in response to companies dominating the market for their products so that they could charge high prices for low quality goods. The companies that formed monopolies included meatpacking, railroads, and other transportation. Monopolies would be run to prevent other businesses from entering the market. We should look at limiting the ability of tech companies to monopolize. At the very least, we need to ensure that tech companies are acting ethically. We need to carefully consider the impact that artificial intelligence (AI) will have on our society. We need to run government sponsored studies to review issues such as AI to ensure our safety.

One example of a restrictive regulation has to do with oil and gas. Biden has curtailed leasing of federal lands for oil and gas. There are many new regulations on the oil and gas industries. (65,66,67) Fighting climate change is important, but I wonder if we are taking a punitive approach to the oil and gas industries. We need to use oil and gas until we find a suitable alternative. We are rushing headlong into green energy, but that technology isn't completely tested. Our environment is important. But people need to be able to put food on their tables. I favor regulations that protect workers and consumers from big business. Consumer safety regulations are an example of good regulations. But sometimes the government can overreach. We need to consider the big picture with our energy needs. We don't need the government to tell us what size soda we can buy. (68) The price of oil is important because it is in everything. Everything uses oil for transportation. Many items have plastic components. Plastic is derived from oil. Any increase in the price of oil will cause an increase in prices. We need to protect people from big business. We need to tax businesses so that they pay their fair share from their profits. But we need businesses to compete and be profitable. We need businesses to be able to compete so that we can tax them.

Sometimes governments charge taxes on items to encourage people to limit consumption. This is called a Pigouvian tax. It was named for economist Arthur Pigou. Governments charge these taxes because they feel that the use of certain goods creates a negative impact on society. (69) Some governments like to charge taxes on gas to limit consumption. Where does this money go? What effect do these taxes have on the economy? I worry that the Pigouvian taxes go into a government slush fund. Government funds should be spent to benefit the people.

Nonsense Workplace Policies

There are several workplace habits that need to end. We can't outlaw these, but we can still demand change. Some cashiers at stores are forced to stand all day. They don't move much. Having cashiers sit on a stool would not hurt their productivity. But workers are forced to stand on their feet all day long because the bosses don't feel people are working unless they are suffering. Standing all day puts undue pressure on employees' feet, legs, and backs. This could cause workers comp issues. But I see no benefit.

It would not hurt employers to let employees have breaks on occasion. Workers are not donkeys. If workers can catch their breath occasionally, they would work better. But some people don't believe that you are working unless you are suffering. The rigid work hours don't help either. I work at least 8-5. When I worked in the office, I felt like I was asking the boss for a big favor when I had to take care of something during business hours. But when would I do personal business? Most places are open only 8-5. Back-to-back meetings are also a bad idea. Many times, people have no idea why they are in a certain meeting. Many feel that they attend too many meetings that waste their time. (70) If you have meetings all day, when do you get any work done?

Dressing up is also a practice that needs to go. Unless the customer or clients meet you, you don't need to dress up. Employees work better when they are comfortable. Conformity is another outdated practice. Limiting hair styles can be a way to discriminate against minorities. Why can't we just be more accepting of people who are different?

There is currently a 'war' going on over returning to the office. Why? If an employee can get more done at home, why must they be at the office all day? Is it so that the bosses can stand over the workers while they work, and have workers stare at their ugly faces all day? I feel like this is more of a control issue. Workers can be more productive at home and face less costs. When I work at home, the time I save from my commute is usually spent working. Rather than having me fume in traffic, the boss gets more work from me. If more people worked from home, they could save gas and reduce their carbon footprint. Remote work can be a great way to help reduce our emissions and fight climate change. But our leaders want to insist that we make the daily slog into the office. Even President Biden is in on this. He called for federal workers to return to the office. Many federal employees were willing to quit or retire. A recent poll suggests that sixty eight percent of employees prefer to work from home at least part time. We should stand up for this right and not just slide back into doing things just because that is how it's always been done. (71, 72)

There are certain beliefs and philosophies that need to be dumped. It is NOT illegal to discuss and compare salaries. Sometimes, companies will keep people working at jobs for years with little to no raises. Then, they hire the new workers at higher wages. This should encourage people to switch jobs on a regular basis. Companies strongly discourage workers from comparing notes because they don't want employees to share information. Maybe that is why some companies don't like to have employees talking to one another during work. The bosses want to be sure that they are the only ones holding the information. Perhaps if employees started talking, they might unionize. We just can't have that.

Key performance indicators are another idea that can turn bad. Sometimes managers will force a KPI on employees because it is their pet project. Maybe companies follow KPIs because other companies are using them. Maybe the data for certain KPIs are easy to collect. I have found that sometimes companies tailor their procedures around their software. Departments will do things because that is what the software allows. This happens even when the software produces results that don't make sense. KPIs are better as indicators rather than targets. If you demand that employees reach KPI targets, you may find that they will surprise you by reaching the KPIs but still failing to meet the needs of the business. Perhaps your police department would target patrolling apartment buildings because each residence counts as a solved case. Maybe you will find that different branches of your store are competing and undercutting each other for the same customers. In Russia, the factories made a target of producing a certain weight of nails. The factory produced tons of larger nails, but you could never find a smaller nail. When the factory changed the KPI to the number of nails, it produced millions of small nails. The factory needed to produce the right quantity of each kind of nail needed. Instead, you had huge surpluses and huge deficits in the production of different kinds of nails. KPIs tend to be targeted with no regard for common sense. (73)

How To Help Small Businesses

Approximately half of Americans work for small businesses. (74) Small businesses were central to Adam Smith's model of capitalism. These businesses would compete to provide better goods and services at lower prices. If we help small businesses, we help American workers.

The best way to help small businesses is to only tax those who profit. We need to reduce the barriers to business and only tax profits. We should only have regulations that protect customers and employees. It is true that a minimum wage and accounting regulations are a burden to small businesses. Sometimes we need to manage competing goals to benefit society. But we should do everything we can to help small businesses while protecting workers. We should remove excess licensing and extensive reporting requirements. It is a balancing act. We need to be sure regulations serve a needed purpose. Businesses need to spend their time making money, not filling out stupid reports. If we keep barriers against businesses, they won't survive very long for us to tax.

We have Sallie Mae to underwrite student loans and Fannie Mae to underwrite mortgages. We should expand the U.S. Small Business Administration to underwrite small business loans. This is a current program that we should support so that small businesses have access to capital. These businesses need more help after the pandemic.

Research and development grants are also a good idea. Worker training programs will help businesses find well trained workers. We need to tax the wealthy so that we can fund these programs. (75)

While we have lost some of the protections we had during the 'Golden Age of Capitalism', our condition isn't as bad as it was over 100 years ago. I have made a list of our ideas to ensure that we don't lose the protections that we have.

Our List of Demands

Raise the minimum wage to a living wage.

Raises taxes on those making more than $500,000 in income.

Raise social security taxes or tax the wealthy to ensure the continued functioning of this program.

Have the federal government host a clearing house and prepare taxes on their servers to simplify taxes.

Provide free education for certain degree programs for gainful employment if grades are maintained.

Expand Medicare so that the underserved can receive medical care.

Review working conditions and consider making paid time off and benefits mandatory.

Use government funds to invest in infrastructure and to provide good paying jobs.

Support unions to ensure workers are protected.

Continue regulations that protect workers and consumers.

Remove regulations that do not protect workers, investors, and consumers.

Remove taxes levied before profit and raise taxes on profit.

Support small businesses where it can be done while protecting workers and consumers.

Remove excessive licensing and reporting requirements for small businesses.

Provide free information that businesses can use to succeed.

Raise tariffs and pushback against countries that aren't committed to fair wages for workers such as China and Mexico.

Remove incentives for companies to send jobs overseas.

Government contracts should be given only to those with workers in the U.S.

CHAPTER NINE

HOW DO WE GET THE CHANGE WE NEED?

CHAPTER NINE

HOW DO WE GET THE CHANGE WE NEED?

Neither the Democrats nor the Republicans have given us what we need. Both parties seem to be committed to neoliberalism. If either party had the answers, we wouldn't have the problems that we do. If the answers were simple and ready to use, our problems would have been solved long ago.

With our current media influence on voting, it's likely that no one in office is truly qualified to lead us. The politicians usually aren't experts, scientists, or thinkers. Politicians only know how to get elected; they don't know anything else. Politicians aren't very original; they will do what others have done before without thinking it through. They aren't experts, they go by polls and conventional wisdom. Some politicians vote for what they believe the voters want. Some vote for ideals inspired by misguided beliefs. Many in office may have been bought off by lobbyists. A few politicians have studied or have experts advising them. There is a definite disconnect between what the politicians propose and what America needs. We need a way to guide those in office so that we can get what we need.

The Republicans are the most vocal proponents of neoliberalism, free trade, and tax breaks for the wealthy. Republicans are known for deregulation. Regulation for the sake of regulation isn't good. But we need to keep laws such as the Dodd Frank act to protect us from reckless investors. Republicans used to be known for fiscal responsibility, but now they have joined the contest to see who can send our national debt the highest. Trump only added to the national debt during his presidency. (1)

But the Democrats haven't done what we need them to do either. It was Bill Clinton (Democrat) who signed NAFTA and gave China favored trade status. (2,3) Clinton is the reason many of our jobs went overseas. It was Joe Biden who was telling us that it was time for us all to go back to working in the office. (4) It seems that all the politicians are busy working for the man. I can't find enough evidence to pin the blame for the hyperinflation on Joe Biden. Joe Biden didn't raise the interest rates. But Biden's gas taxes and energy policy did not help inflation. (5) Since gas is used to transport everything, a tax on gas becomes a tax on everything.

Many Democratic candidates appear to think that we need protection from ourselves. While I criticize the Republicans for not regulating, the Democrats tend to overregulate. They are the ones who would push electric vehicles on us without ensuring that we will be able to use them. They are the ones who want to limit the soda we drink. While we need to raise taxes on the wealthy, we need to hold the government accountable for how it spends our money. My main objection to a carbon tax is that I don't know where the money will be spent. The carbon tax would also be a barrier to making a profit. We want to keep businesses running so we can tax their profits. We need to oversee the government and demand that they spend the money taxed for our benefit. Any regulation that we pass should be reviewed later to ensure that the law is providing the results we intended.

Clearly, our politicians need our guidance. This is the principal reason that we need to become more vocal than ever. There are many ways that we can provide guidance and we need to let them know what we need. I've noticed there is often a disconnect between what companies produce and what we need. There is also a disconnect between what politicians propose and what we need. We would benefit if we could bridge this divide.

VOTE

The most important action you can take is to vote. Many people leave their vote on the table and remain silent. Approximately one third of eligible citizens did not vote in the last presidential election. (6) It's important to make your voice heard. Not only should you vote in the presidential elections, but you should also vote in primaries and off year elections. The primary elections help to determine the candidates who will run for president, congress, and the local offices. Vocally support your favorite candidate. You can donate to your candidate, but you shouldn't feel pressure to do so. Primaries help shape the issues. You can help pick the candidate your party will choose for the final election.

The president doesn't run the country alone. The president must cooperate with the Senate and the House of Representatives. If the federal government doesn't address an issue, perhaps your governor or state congress can help. While the national minimum wage is $7.25, Michigan has set their minimum wage at $10 per hour. (7) Sometimes your state will address issues that the federal government doesn't. That's why it's important to vote responsibly down the line. The attention given to a president should be given to every level of government. Any issues should be taken up with the White House and the local governments. Local officials will provide more access and attention to your concerns.

Why Vote?

If you don't vote, you don't get a chance to help decide the fate of this country. The right is free and involves showing up with proof that you are a citizen. Some people in this country may want to make it more difficult to vote. You should vote now to prevent these people from interfering with your right to vote.

Voting is a civilized way to address issues. With a monarchy or dictatorship, nobody cares what you think. You have no voice. The government works specifically for those in charge and not for the citizens. The only way to change things in a dictatorship is through bloody and violent revolution. But in a democracy, violence is not needed. In fact, violence is a barrier to resolving the issues. Was anything resolved in the attack on the Capitol in January 2021? We have a system that was tailor made to allow us to address issues without violence. We are in charge, and we can make the government work for the people. But we need to be involved!

The Electoral College – Why?

In at least two elections, candidates managed to win without getting the majority of the popular vote. George W. Bush lost the popular vote but had most of the electoral votes. (8) Donald Trump won over Hilary Clinton because he had most of the electoral votes. But he lost the popular vote by over 2.8 million votes! (9) How did this happen? This came about from the rules of the Electoral College. Each state is awarded a certain number of electoral votes based on the population of the state. When we vote, we don't vote for the candidate directly. We vote for a representative at the Electoral College. If the candidate wins the majority of the votes in a state, their group sends their representatives to vote at the college. Winner takes all for each state. (10)

How is it possible that a candidate can win the most votes, and still lose? The short answer is that this is a numbers game. If you don't want to read through the math, you can skip to the next paragraph. This involves a complicated story problem. We all loved those in grade school. Here is my example. Let's say you have 100 people voting for whether to paint the hall red or blue. Each room would represent a state. The largest room has 40 people but 32 of them vote for blue. With the Electoral College, all 40 of those votes would go towards blue even if 8 people voted for red. Let's say that we have five other rooms with 12 people. Each of these rooms had 8 people vote for red and 4 people vote for blue per room. With the rules, these other five rooms would use their votes to choose red for a total of 60 votes going to red. So, the hall would be painted red. In this case, we had a total of 48 people voting for red and 52 people voting for blue. We had 32 people in the largest room vote for blue and 4 people from 5 other rooms adding 20 votes for blue. This totals 52. This is the majority, yet the minority of the total gets its way. And the majority is unhappy.

Why would we put in such a system? Our system of elections was designed by compromise. Some of our founding fathers wanted representation by population. Others wanted representation by state. So, our House of Representatives is represented by population, but each state gets two senators regardless of population. In the Senate, Rhode Island has the same number of representatives as California.

This is true even though California is a much bigger state. The founding fathers wanted to avoid the 'tyranny of the majority'. (11) One example I read was that we would not want the majority to rule that the Great Lake states should send all their water to the Southwest. The idea was that the minority vote has a voice. We must decide for ourselves what is right. Should we keep this system to protect the minority vote? Or is it outdated or just plain wrong? Either way, we are in charge.

If enough of us want it, we can abolish the Electoral College. We can amend the constitution! We've done it before, and we will do it again. An amendment can be proposed if two thirds of both Houses of Congress agree to make an amendment. Two thirds of the states can also call for a convention to amend the Constitution. If three quarters of the states ratify the amendment, then the Electoral College is history! (12) The problem is that the party in the majority isn't likely to remove the process that may have helped them win the election. Maine and Nebraska do not have a winner take all approach. They use a proportional representation approach. So, we may be able to lobby our states to change the rules. If we change how most of the states operate, we can make the electoral college more closely match the popular vote. (10)

How did we get the two-party system?

Early in the United States, there were two opposing views on how to handle foreign relations and the role of the federal government. There were opposing views of George Washington versus Thomas Jefferson. Later, the views were divided between the North and the South. The parties weren't as organized as they are today. The parties evolved based on the interests of the people. Jefferson led the Democratic Republicans which eventually became just the Democrats by 1820. The Republicans replaced the Whig Party by the 1850s. The two parties that we have today been here for over 150 years. The issues in previous years tended to be fewer. How should we handle foreign relations with Europe? Should we have a centralist federal government, or should we have a confederation of states? Should we keep slavery, or should we abolish it? Before the Civil War, the interests were often separated by the North versus the South. Our issues are more complex today. How should we stimulate the economy? What role should the government have in the economy? What should the government do to protect the environment? Does the government need to protect the people from themselves? What should our stance be on gun control? Should abortion be legal? What should our foreign policy be? How aggressive should we pursue our interest abroad? There are many more complex issues due to our times and the size of our nation. Since our two political parties have been national institutions for over one hundred and fifty years, it is unlikely we will have a strong third party. (13)

Multiple Parties

I find that our two-party system fits our country like a cheap suit. I despise trickle-down economics. I want workers to be protected. But I don't like the 'nanny state' that the Democrats want to create. We need protection from Big Business. We need someone to pool our resources together to provide infrastructure, defense, and other public goods that we can't provide for ourselves. Other than that, leave us alone!

It seems these days that we are becoming more and more polarized. (14) Our candidates tend to represent the most extreme versions of our views. Maybe our media promotes those who make the most noise. It sounds sensible that the best government is boring. But a boring government does not get ratings. Boring candidates do not get attention even if they are the most qualified.

In some European countries, they have ranked choice voting. (15) Let's say you have Bernie Sanders, Hilary Clinton, Joseph Biden, Donald Trump, Nikki Haley, and Mike Pence on the ballot. You would choose your top three favorite candidates. If the first choice wins the majority, they win. If not, the primary votes of the least favorite primary candidate have the secondary choice go towards the primary choice. The voting system would keep going until one candidate wins a clear majority. If one of the candidates could get some of the votes from everyone, they might win. This might solve our extremism problem. Perhaps we could then all agree on a candidate that we don't mind sitting in office. We may even find that independent candidates would win more often. In a poll published in 2023, 43% of voters identified as independent. (16) With our "winner take all" approach, one side is happy, but the other side is dissatisfied. With our Electoral College, it is possible that the majority may be dissatisfied.

Sometimes I feel like voting for 'none of the above'. I would do that if it was an option. Richard Pryor starred in a movie titled Brewster's Millions. He had to spend $30 million in 30 days to inherit $300 million. He spent the money to run on a campaign for 'none of the above'. None of the candidates on the ballot were truly qualified.

We need to work harder to get our voices heard. We can either contact our candidates in our party or provide more support for third party choices. In the UK, there are many more parties. While the Conservative and Unionist Party and the Labour Party both dominate, there are as many as twelve different parties in the House of Commons. (17) I would say that their more complex system is better at representing the voices of the voters. More parties allow for more nuances for the issues. It is more likely that each issue of the people will be represented. With our two-party system, I feel that I must choose which issues are more important and just accept that other issues will be handled poorly.

Contact Your Leaders

A good way to make your voice heard is to contact your representatives in office. Many people are uninvolved, so calling or writing your leaders allows you to have influence that others don't. Often, you will get a response about your concern. Letters and email are best because the staff is better able to handle written communications. Calls are likely to be handled by staff who are not prepared to answer your concern. Letters and email are a good way to contact your representatives privately. Facebook, X(Twitter), and other social media can be a way to post your concern publicly. What you post on social media can be seen by others who see it. You can always encourage others to post so that your representative can see that you have numbers on your side. But some government officials will have limited exposure to social media because they have been trolled. When contacting representatives directly, it's good to remain polite and keep to the facts.

Here are a few tips to write effectively. Try to keep the letter clear and concise. Stick to one issue. It is best to start out polite and stick to the point. One-page letters work best. Try to provide some details about who you are and how the issue will affect you. Use facts to back up your requests and opinions. Be clear about what you expect from your representative. If time is of the essence, email is best. You may even want to contact candidates during an election so that they will know the issues that are important to the public. Candidates are especially attentive during elections.

You may even be able to meet one of your representatives. While you probably can't meet with the president, you should be able to arrange a meeting with a member of Congress. As the representatives become more local, it's more likely that you can arrange a meeting. Many politicians have local offices where you can arrange a meeting with the representative or a member of their staff. Remember to keep it polite and do your best to maintain your credibility. (18)

Recalling Elected Officials

Perhaps you would like to recall an official that is doing a bad job. That may be more difficult than you expect. Recalling refers to the process of holding another election to replace a current official. If enough people sign a petition for a recall for a state official, then the state will hold a recall election. Most states do not allow recalls. This is specified by the state's constitution. Only nineteen states have provisions for recalling an official. (19) Presidents cannot be recalled. They must be impeached. First, the House of Representatives brings charges to impeach. If a majority of the House votes to impeach, the Senate holds a trial. If the majority of the Senate votes to impeach, the official is removed from office. After impeachment, they may never run for office again. Presidents, senators, representatives, and officials can be impeached. Governors and state officials can be impeached by their state legislature. (20) According to the twenty fifth amendment, the vice president would take over if a president is impeached. The line of succession works the same whether a president is impeached or becomes unable to fulfill the duties of the office. (21)

Social Media

There is no shortage of political activity on social media. Everyone wants to be a political commentator. Without an organization, our posts may not go very far. Without facts, our posts are likely to have limited impact. Most politicians limit their postings on social media. It's very easy to have their words used against them. It's very easy to collect a string of negative comments. It's less important to post on social media than it is to gather lots of followers. It's not enough to act, we need to get organized! Once you have many followers, you can encourage them to act!

Get Organized

If we want change, we need to organize! One of the issues movements has had is longevity. Many protesters start with campaigns ready to change the world. But after a few weeks, life goes back to normal. Change is a marathon rather than a sprint. Saul Alinsky would say that "A tactic that drags on too long becomes a drag." (22) Many may think that if we hold a few brilliantly organized protests, we can make immediate change. Much change has been slow and gradual in nature. We must develop long term relationships and organizations to make lasting change. The visible activities of activists might be voting drives, protests, writing emails, meetings, and sending petitions. When you think of activism, you might think of mass protests. But much of the work is developing connections and member lists so that you can draw a large crowd to your protest. In 2023, Shawn Fain and the UAW selectively picked sites to strike rather than striking everyplace at once. (23) This allowed him to get his message across for longer in a way that the UAW would be less likely to deplete its strike fund. We must take a long and slow approach. Do a little bit every now and then. Keep a member list. We might stage a single protest when an official is in town. In this case, we would be using strategy. We don't want to stage a massive weeks-long protest. We would want to stage a protest when we know a candidate is in town so that we can send a message. Of course, we would keep our protest legal and non-violent. Perhaps a later, a group could encourage its members to contact a particular congress person.

Expectations & Strategy

We must face the fact that we may not be able to get everything we want. But we can still make a difference. The political response to Occupy Wall Street was underwhelming. But it did set the narrative for the 99%. This book is even inspired by the narrative of the 99% versus the 1% who wish to oppress them. The 1% hold most of the wealth and they are using that wealth to oppress everyone. (24) Since there are so many viewpoints, we will never get everyone to agree. But we only need to get enough people to form a majority to make a change.

Our goals would be to convince enough people to vote for our favorite candidates and then convince our elected officials to vote for legislation that benefits us. Part of organizing may be to form a voting bloc. We can organize the election of our favorite candidate around which candidate will give us the most of what we want. We can also communicate what we want so that the elected officials know what we want. In effect, we can become community-based lobbyists. We convince our officials to vote on our behalf. We can use the size of our organization to leverage votes and make change for the better. Fighting for change can be exhausting. That is why we need to use strategy to minimize our effort and maximize our impact. We may not be able to convince everyone to vote on our behalf. If our representatives don't agree with us, we can always reach out to other officials who do. Perhaps we have a Senator who does not want to raise the minimum wage. Maybe our representative in the House will help us. If we can't get the federal government to raise the wage, we may be able to get our raise passed through the State Senate. You are unlikely to get an official to vote against their core beliefs. But you may be able to sway the minds of the undecided or those in the middle. Try not to burn any bridges. A politician who votes against you on one issue may vote with you on another issue.

We can use protests to raise awareness and show the number of people who support our cause. We can use letter writing campaigns to show the politicians that we have numbers on our size. We can use our member lists to help with voting drives, signing petitions, and raising awareness. But we must organize to make the most use of our resources. The best strategy would be to have a few key people negotiate on behalf of the people. These people would talk to officials. They would direct votes, protests, and letter writing campaigns. These few people would do the heavy lifting. The members would only be asked to get involved a few times out of the year. But it should be done in a way to maximize the impact of the organization. Our efforts should be targeted and planned.

The Art of Persuasion and Organizational Motivation

I came across an article about persuasion that I wanted to include about persuasion and motivation. The first tip was to do someone a favor before you ask them for something. The example stated that if you start a task, you are more likely to get them to finish the task. It is easier than having them complete the entire task. As an organization, it would be good to explain what has been done to get the ball rolling. Perhaps you know an official will be in town, but you need people to show up for an afternoon to let the official know that you mean business. People want to know that you have made an investment in what you are asking them to do. Another tip is to ask for a smaller favor first. Sometimes, you can get people to like you if you ask for something. The other person feels like they have an investment in you.

When organizing, it's good to explain to everyone why they are helping you. Why do you need them to show up? What will they gain if they help you? If you are fighting to raise the minimum wage, you can let people know that many will get a raise if you win. Perhaps you can appeal to your members' sense of fairness. Or you can remind them that they are helping to make the world a fairer place. Sometimes people will need to be told what they gain from helping you.

Another idea is to let people think that helping you is their idea. On a personal level, you might talk about charity and helping people. Then you would mention you have a daughter who is working on a fundraiser. The hope is that the other person would volunteer to give or help on their own. This might be more difficult from an organization. It's best for an organization to be direct with its members.

Talking about what people will lose is another tactic. Perhaps you could say that there is an opportunity to put the minimum wage up to a vote. This opportunity will be lost if there isn't enough support. People will often respond more to what they lose than what they could gain.

Ask people to do things that are consistent with who they are. You are unlikely to get an NRA member to attend a protest for gun control. However, raising the minimum wage is likely to help people of color the most. So, those who support equality would also support raising the minimum wage. This is where a coalition comes in. Those who support Black Lives Matter would likely support raising the minimum wage. But not everyone in one group has been reached by the second group. But if the two organizations work together, the members can use the extra numbers to support actions that are likely to benefit everyone in the two groups. If a person acts to support a cause in the past, they will do so in the future. If they signed up for your email list and signed your petition, they are more likely to show up for a protest.

Pay attention to what the other person wants. Listen. Let your members have input in what the organization does. Be clear about what you are planning to do and try to work for what your members want. If people know that you are listening to them, it will make a difference.

Use numbers to your advantage. You can phrase requests in a way to let them know that all the cool kids are doing it. This may be a manner of presentation. For instance, you could say that you expect there will be a huge turnout. Perhaps as many as 5,000 people for example.

Use "we". We are doing everything. You want the members to feel that they are included in the group. Remind them that you are working for a common cause. Remind everyone that we are all in this together. As Benjamin Franklin once said, "If we don't hang together, we will surely hang separately." Emphasize the shared bond that the organization has through working together. (25)

Give the person something before you ask them. Some people feel the need to reciprocate. Perhaps a small gift will convince people to help you. There may not be the funds to do this for an organization.

Ask for more than what you want. For an organization, it may be better to just be clear about what you are expecting. Perhaps you could talk about what was done in the past. Talk about the extra effort that had to be put in. The members will think that you are asking them to do something difficult. They will be relieved when you ask for something smaller.

If you review the counter arguments, this may strengthen your argument. Let people know that you have looked at both sides of the argument. You can make the counter arguments available as a resource so that your members can use them when they talk to people.

Be sure to appear to ethos, pathos, and logos in your argument. Ethos supports credibility. Why should people believe you? Use any certifications that you have personally. Use sources to back up your arguments. Pathos appeals to your emotions. For instance, it is unfair that the minimum wage hasn't been raised in 15 years. It is unfair that people work 40 plus hours and have to apply for public benefits. Logos involves logic. A person must be able to make enough money to pay their bills. Otherwise, people will default on their bills. Paying bills on time keeps society running. If enough people fail to earn enough to pay their bills, society will suffer.

When possible, make people laugh. This is better as a personal tool to persuade someone. Start out with a conversation. Form a bond. Then make the ask. For organizations, maybe it is a good idea to make functions fun. If meetings are fun, people will attend. If protests have food and music, they won't be so much of a chore. It's easier to work together if a group has fun together. This is easier to do if protests are short, targeted events rather than a drawn-out campaign.

Get members in the habit of agreeing with you. This is where an organization would remind people of items where they agree. If people are in the streak of agreeing, they don't want to break the momentum.

Being persistent can help. But don't be annoying or aggressive. Maybe you can ask people about multiple issues. Politics is complicated. Maybe you can't get someone to act on one issue. Maybe they care about another. Once they take action with you on one issue, they are more likely to take action again.

Make every contact with your members positive. Express your faith that the members care about the world around them, so you just know they will come through for you. We are a powerful organization that prides itself on coming together to make a difference. We're going to change the world.

Let your members know the urgency of the issues. Make the stakes well known. People are more likely to act if they feel an issue is urgent. Perhaps you can ask for a commitment by a certain time so that you can organize appropriately.

Always project confidence. If you are an organization leader, you are in charge. You may have doubts, but don't express those doubts when you are calling for action. You are on a mission. You are set out to change the world! There's no room for doubts when you are setting out to change the world.

Lastly, be sure to respect your members and the cost of their time. Always do whatever you can to maximize the impact they can have. Keep the burden as light as possible. Don't make activism a second job. Remember that the members are sacrificing their time and even money to further the shared agenda. Make the members glad they made the sacrifice. When you win, be sure to remind the members about the impact of what they have gained so they can feel good about what they have done. (26)

Battling Businesses

It's not only politicians who need to change. We need to show businesses that we won't take their shenanigans anymore. We can organize politically to establish legislation. We can organize the use of our dollars to show the businesses that they don't want to make us unhappy. We can support businesses who do the right thing. We can withhold support from businesses who act in unethical manners.

Why should we get involved in businesses? Shouldn't companies run their operations in a way that makes the most profit? Milton Friedman certainly thought so. (Friedman, p 133) He wrote that businesses should only concern themselves with making a profit. You might say that sounds fair. But then, as Americans, we are free to act in our own best interests. I argue that it is in our best interest to limit what corporations can do. We can use our vote and we can use our dollar. It is only fair that we do what makes our lives better. It is only fair that we work to make society work for us. The 99%.

I have read about people being canceled for making racist, sexist, or homophobic comments on Facebook. There are instances of people being canceled for being filmed acting in racist ways. Actors have had shows canceled because of remarks they have made. Why can't we cancel executives who make policies that hurt people? I suggest that we cancel the next executive who demands the employees go back to the office. At the very least, we can organize a boycott if a company does something that we feel is wrong. (27)

You may wonder how we can possibly boycott all businesses that are in the wrong. We must do business with someone. We can't stop shopping. I suggest that if we have an industry that acts unethically, we just pick one to boycott. It doesn't matter which company we choose. If it is possible for one company to face a backlash for taking an unethical action, then all companies are likely to avoid that action. We want to send a message that certain actions aren't tolerated. We start with one company; the competition could be next. It doesn't matter if all competitors in an industry are guilty. The idea is to establish an extra risk for unethical behavior. The idea is that if you act unethically, you will face consequences. We need to organize to become a power block and show the 1% that they don't want to mess with us.

Decades ago, a woman won a million-dollar settlement from McDonald's because she burned herself drinking their coffee. I've read that the coffee was scalding hot. The woman was elderly and had third degree burns from the coffee. She spent months in the hospital. But the point is, companies hear about these events, and they remember. Now, you can't get any coffee without a warning telling you the obvious fact that the coffee is hot. (28)

In Rules for Radicals, Saul Alinsky had a very interesting tactic for corporate reform. What if we each bought a share of stock. We could use our share to vote and have time on the floor. We could access the shareholder meetings with our shares. We might be able to change how companies operate from the inside. If at least 10% of the shareholders band together, they could call a special meeting. Michael Moore tried to talk to Roger Smith at a shareholder meeting in Roger & Me. He had a 'microphone malfunction'. But I don't think that would happen if thousands were to show up at the meeting. We would have to make sure to vote our shares and use those shares to make a change. We would have to make the votes ourselves. Sometimes, stocks offer to have you vote by proxy. One option is to have an organization hold proxy votes to make a change. (22, 29)

Support Local Businesses

We can always support local businesses. Local businesses use American workers, and the money tends to stay in the country. Those who run local businesses tend to be normal everyday people. Small businesses may try harder. Large corporations may send their money to any place in the world. Mega corporations may outsource their workforce to other countries. Large corporations aren't evil by definition. Some large corporations are ethical. Amazon treats its customers very well and buys from many small businesses. You can sell products as a business from your home if you choose. But we need to let big business know that we won't tolerate mistreatment.

Forming a Union

You can form a union if you would like. It's not easy but it can be done. Unions can provide better wages and benefits. Unions allow workers to negotiate as a block so that all workers are treated fairly. Unions provide protection and will address grievances for workers. If you can find enough coworkers who are truly unhappy with the way management is treating them, you can form a union and make changes!

Your employer can't penalize you for attempting to form a union. (30) If a company tries to punish you for forming a union, you should contact your state's Department of Labor. But you need to organize outside of company hours and off company premises. There is no size limit to unions. You can have as few as two people in a union if they form the majority. A petition or union card count of 30% of the workforce will allow you to formalize a vote. You would start by having employees sign a card to state their preference. Once you have support of at least 30%, you have more legal protections. You want to be careful in the beginning so that management doesn't try to come up with reasons to terminate you that are unrelated to forming a union. A vote of 50% plus one allows you to form a union. You may find that there is a pre-existing union you can join. You will want to check the local laws and ask other unions for advice near the beginning of your process. There are union organizations that can provide advice and support.

The first step is to get a list of employees who are sympathetic to a union. Avoid coworkers who are against unions, friends of management, or in management. Try to talk to employees face to face. Don't use email or text. Once you get enough people willing to join, you can start holding meetings and form a committee. Once you find that you have enough support, you will want to see if you can join a pre-existing union. Most unions are based in a state. So, you would look for a union in your state. You will also want to review the laws regarding unions for your state. For instance, if you are a teacher, you can join a teachers' union. You may be able to contact the AFL-CIO for an organizer and advice. If you can get more than 50% of the workforce on board, the company must negotiate with you. (31,32,33)

Final Thoughts

We can either let society continue to slide as it has, or we can take action. We need to let the politicians know that we are watching. We are the voting public, and it is up to us to decide the kind of country we want to have. We need to let the business leaders know that there are rules. We are the consumer, and the businesses need our dollars. If we band together, we can make the world a better place for ourselves and our families. You have the power! Now it is time to put down this book, get up, go, and fight for change.

AFTERWORD
RIGHTS YOU MAY NOT KNOW YOU HAVE

It's important to know what rights you have. You can't just assume that your boss or employer will know and follow the laws. Your workplace should have a poster displayed that lists some of your rights. You should learn about the rights that you have. Not all business owners know the rights, and some will try to deny your rights to save a buck. This happens more often than you would think.

I worked in a company that had a problem with employees arriving late for their shifts. A memo was going to go out stating that if an employee was late, the company would not pay them for the first fifteen minutes they were working. I was able to read a copy of the memo a few days before it was sent out. So, I confirmed with the Department of Labor that my company's plan was illegal. When I received the memo, I told the owner and the manager that they could not legally withhold pay for time worked. The manager replied that other companies had done that before. I told them that just because other companies do something, that does not mean that it is legal. The company did not follow through with their plan. If you feel that your rights are being violated, you can always contact the Department of Labor for your state. You may be able to file a complaint.

The Fair Labor Standards Act establishes minimum wage, overtime pay, recordkeeping, and payment of wages. The minimum wage is $7.25 per hour as of July 2009. One notable exception is that tipped employees can be paid $2.13 per hour as long as their tips for the pay period add up to at least the minimum wage for the time they worked. But for non-exempt workers, your employer must pay at least the minimum wage. If the state has a higher minimum wage, then the employer must use that amount instead. (1) If you work more than 40 hours in a week, you are entitled to be paid a rate that is at least one and a half times your regular rate for 'overtime'. There are a few exceptions. You must actually be working over 40 hours in order to qualify for overtime for that pay period. If you are paid 8 hours for holiday pay and work an extra 42 hours throughout the week, you are only eligible for time and a half for the 2 hours you worked over 40 hours. This is true even if you are being paid for 50 hours with holiday pay. Exempt employees are those who receive a salary over $35,568 per year and are considered professional, administrative, or executive. Exempt employees are salaried and do not receive extra compensation for hours worked over 40 in a week. (2) You must be paid for all the time that you are required to be on the premises of your workplace. This would include waiting time. It is your manager's responsibility to ensure that you stop working after your shift is done. If you continue working, you must be paid for the time you worked. As an employee, you are legally unable to waive these rights. This was put into place so that your boss couldn't force you to waive your right to overtime pay.

Your employer must pay you regularly on the appointed paydays. Unless the payday falls on a holiday, you may be able to file a claim with the Department of Labor if your employer pays late. If you leave your job, your employer must pay your last paycheck by the appointed payday. You are entitled to any vacation pay that you have accrued.

Some businesses attempt to save money on taxes and benefits by classifying people as independent contractors rather than employees. There are serious penalties for misclassifying employees including back payment of taxes. The Internal Revenue Service (IRS) may apply interest and penalties. There are several questions to be asked to determine the difference. How much control does the person have over their work? If the employer sets the hours, place, and tasks, then the person is an employee. Does the company train the person? If so, they may be an employee. How often and how is the person paid? If they are paid like an employee, then they may be an employee. This classification is important to the employee because it determines whether the employer or the employee pays the employer taxes. As an employee, the company is liable for benefits, insurance, and certain payroll taxes. If you are an independent contractor, you pay for your own benefits, payroll taxes, and insurances required. (3, 4)

If you leave your job and your employer has more than 20 employees, you are eligible to continue your employer sponsored healthcare plan for at least 18 months. This is called COBRA and it was a law passed called the Consolidated Omnibus Budget Reconciliation Act. You should receive a COBRA letter informing you of your right to continue medical coverage within 30 days after you leave the company. The company has the right to charge 102% of the medical coverage premiums. The extra 2% is for administrative expenses. (5)

If a company has 50 or more full-time employees, they must offer a healthcare plan. This applies to full time equivalents (FTE). So, if a company has 25 full time employees and 50 part time employees working 20 hours per week, they will have to offer health insurance to their full-time employees because they have at least 50 FTEs. Employees who work more than 30 hours per week are considered full time for the purpose of health care enrollment. (6)

The Family Medical Leave Act (FMLA) allows employees 12 weeks a year of unpaid leave if they or a family member has a medical condition. The employer must still provide health insurance during the leave. Employers can't terminate an employee for taking their time off. Reasons for FMLA include the birth or adoption of a child, time off to care for a family member, or a medical condition for the employee. Employees are eligible for FMLA if they have worked for the company for at least a year and the company employs 50 or more people within 75 miles of the employee's workplace. (7)

You have the right to a safe workplace. If your employer refuses to fix a safety issue, you can contact OSHA (Occupational Safety and Health Administration). You have the right to safety training and safe work equipment. You can refuse to work in a situation that will expose you to a hazard. You can request an OSHA inspection if you feel that your workplace is unsafe. You can't be fired or demoted for filing an OSHA complaint. You are protected under the whistleblower laws. (8) Different states have different rules regarding Workers Compensation Insurance. Generally, if a worksite has at least 5 full time employees, they are required to have Workers Comp. If a worker is injured on the job, Workers Comp will pay for the workers' wages and medical bills for the time they are unable to work due to an injury on the job. (9,10)

Most employment in the United States is 'at will' employment. This means that you or your employer can terminate your employment for almost any reason. While it is custom to give two weeks' notice in a professional setting, you can legally just quit. Your boss can generally terminate your employment without notice. If your boss fired you for a reason that is due to discrimination, you will be able to file a wrongful termination suit against them. If you win a wrongful termination suit, you can force your previous employer to pay for lost wages and legal costs. The judge may award punitive damages which may result in a substantial payout. You cannot be discriminated against due to race, Nationality, gender, sexual orientation, gender identity, religion, age, or disability. If you have a disability, your employer is required to make reasonable accommodations so that you can work. You can't be fired in retaliation for reporting a violation or filing a complaint with the Department of Labor. (11)

You have the right to a workplace free from discrimination or harassment. Harassment includes offensive jokes, name calling, physical assaults and threats, and intimidation. If you feel you are being harassed, your manager has a duty to resolve the issue. You have the right to a workplace free from sexual harassment. Sexual harassment includes jokes and unwanted comments. If your employer does not resolve the issue, you can file a complaint and sue them. You have the right to work in a non-hostile work environment. (12)

If you are terminated from your job by your employer, you may be eligible for unemployment payments. If you voluntarily leave your job, you probably won't be eligible for unemployment payments. An exception to that rule involves constructive discharge. Constructive discharge involves a situation where your work environment is so dangerous or hostile that no reasonable person would continue working there. Examples include dangerous conditions or harassment. If you can prove constructive discharge, you may be able to win a suit for wrongful termination. (13,14)

It is important to stand up for your rights. Knowledge is power. The Department of Labor can provide valuable information and assistance. They can help you to decide whether you should file a claim for damages if your rights have been violated. If in doubt, pick up the phone and call them.

NOTES

FOREWORD

1.Issie Lapowsky, Millions of People Checked Out Clinton's Debate Fact-Check Site, WIRED, September 27, 2016,
https://www.wired.com/2016/09/millions-people-fact-checked-debate-clintons-website/
2.Internet Encyclopedia of Philosophy, Plato, Retrieved January 26,2024,
https://iep.utm.edu/plato/
3.MasterClass, Plato's Allegory of the Cave Explained, masterclass.com,
October 23, 2022, https://www.masterclass.com/articles/allegory-of-the-cave-explainede
4.Eric Bradner, Conway: Trump White House offered 'alternative facts' on crowd size, CNN, January 23, 2017,
 https://www.cnn.com/2017/01/22/politics/kellyanne-conway-alternative-facts/index.html
5.Jane C. Timm, Trump signs tax cut bill, first big legislative win, NBC News, December 22, 2017,
https://www.nbcnews.com/politics/politics-news/trump-signs-tax-cut-bill-first-big-legislative-win-n832141
6.David Floyd, Explaining the Trump Tax Reform Plan, Investopedia, January 23, 2023,
https://www.investopedia.com/taxes/trumps-tax-reform-plan-explained/
7.U.S. Department of Labor, History of Federal Minimum Wage Rates Under the Fair Labor Standards Act, 1938 - 2009,
https://www.dol.gov/agencies/whd/minimum-wage/history/chart
8.Scott Horsley, Inflation has cooled a lot. So why do things still feel so expensive?, NPR, December 16, 2023,
https://www.npr.org/2023/12/16/1219574403/economy-inflation-prices-wages-disinflation-deflation-interest-rate
9.Rob Wile, Federal Reserve raises key interest rate to highest level in more than 20 years, NBC News, July 26, 2023,
https://www.nbcnews.com/business/economy/interest-rate-hike-july-2023-how-much-higher-federal-reserve-rcna96210
10.Federal Reserve, Jerome H. Powell, Federal Reserve History Page, Retrieved January 26, 2024,
https://www.federalreservehistory.org/people/jerome-h-powell

11.Environmental Protection Agency, Biden-Harris Administration Finalizes Standards to Slash Methane Pollution, Combat Climate Change, Protect Health, and Bolster American Innovation, EPA.gov, December 2, 2023, https://www.epa.gov/newsreleases/biden-harris-administration-finalizes-standards-slash-methane-pollution-combat-climate
12.Renee Valdes, How Long Does It Take To Charge An Electric Car?, Kelley Blue Book, July 11, 2023, https://www.kbb.com/car-advice/how-long-does-take-charge-electric-car/
13.Alina Bradford, Ashley Hamer, What is a scientific theory, LiveScience, January 31, 2022, https://www.livescience.com/21491-what-is-a-scientific-theory-definition-of-theory.html

CHAPTER ONE

1.Daniel Lende, Neuroanthropology, The American Reality Versus The American Dream, December, 22, 2007, https://neuroanthropology.net/2007/12/22/the-american-reality-versus-the-american-dream/

2.Ari Shapiro, NPR, American Dream Faces Harsh New Reality, May, 29, 2012, https://www.npr.org/2012/05/29/153513153/american-dream-faces-harsh-new-reality

3.Adam Barone, What Is the American Dream? Examples and How to Measure It, Investopedia, March 28, 2023, https://www.investopedia.com/terms/a/american-dream.asp

4.Lawrence Mishel, Elise Gould, & Josh Bivens, Wage Stagnation in Nine Charts, Economic Policy Institute, January 6, 2015, https://www.epi.org/publication/charting-wage-stagnation/

5.Forbes, Forbes Billionaire List, https://www.forbes.com/billionaires/

CHAPTER TWO

1.Zach Schonfeld, The Hill, Sanders Has Highest Favorability Amount Possible 2024 Contenders Poll, August, 26, 2022, https://thehill.com/homenews/campaign/3617170-sanders-has-highest-favorability-among-possible-2024-contenders-poll/

2.Felix Salmon, "Gen Z Prefers 'Socialism' to 'Capitalism,'" AXIOS, January 27, 2019, https://www.axios.com

3.Emma Green, "Bernie Sanders's Religious Text for Christians in Public Office," The Atlantic, June 8, 2017, https://www.theatlantic.com/politics/archive/2017,06/bernie-sanders-chris-van-hollen-russell-vought/529614/.

4.Merriam-Webster, 2003, https://www.merriam-webster.com/dictionary/socialism

5.Merriam-Webster, 2003 , https://www.merriam-webster.com/dictionary/communism

6.Karl Marx & Frederick Engels, Manifesto of the Communist Party, Moscow, 1848, Marxist Internet Archive (marxists.org) 1987, 2000, 2010. Creative Commons Attribution-Share-Alike License

7.Library of Congress, America at Work, Library of Congress Archives, https://www.loc.gov/collections/america-at-work-and-leisure-1894-to-1915/articles-and-essays/america-at-work

8.Rosanne Tomyn, What were the work conditions in factories in 1900?, Classroom Synonym, June 25, 2018, https://classroom.synonym.com/unique-industrial-revolution-21937.html

9.Andrew Beattie, A History of U.S. Monopolies, Investopedia, September 11, 2022, https://www.investopedia.com/insights/history-of-us-monopolies/

10.U.S. Department of Labor, History of Changes to the Minimum Wage Law, https://www.dol.gov/agencies/whd/minimum-wage/history

11.Dane Hamilton, Jim Cramer Draws Fire Over Manipulation Comments, REUTERS, March 20, 2007, https://www.reuters.com/article/cramer-interview/jim-cramer-draws-fire-over-manipulation-comments-idUKN20362926202007032 0

12.Kim Supermutt Goodman, Preying On Poor People Is The Basis Of Many Local Businesses, NEOCH, May 23, 2016, https://www.neoch.org/chronicle-231articles/2016/5/23/preying-on-poor-people-is-the-basis-of-many-local-businesses.html

13.Kengor, The Devil and Karl Marx, 72.

14.Sarah Cook, The Chinese Communist Party's Latest Propaganda Target: Young Minds, Perspective, (Freedom House), April 30, 2019, https://freedomhouse.org/article/chinese-communist-partys-latest-propaganda-target-young-minds

15. Patrick J. Buchanan, Suicide of a Superpower (New York, NY: Thomas Dunne Books, 2011),207.

16. Anne Applebaum, Iron Curtain: The Crushing of Eastern Europe, 1944-1956 (New York, NY: Khopf Doubleday Publishing Group, 2012), Kindle Edition

17. Rod Dreher, Live Not by Lies, A Manual for Christian Dissidents (New York, NY: Sentinel, 2020),8.

18. George Orwell, Nineteen Eighty-Four, 2021 (Chicago, Penguin Clothbound Classics)

19. Iain Murray in "The Temptation of Socialism: A Conversation with Economist Iain." Thinking in Public, February 1, 2021, https://albertmohler.com/2021/02/01/iain-murray.

20. Brinley Hinaman, Fact check: Socialist policies alone did not destroy Venezuela's economy in the last decade, USA Today, August 8, 2020, https://www.usatoday.com/story/news/factcheck/2020/08/08/fact-check-socialism-alone-did-not-destroy-venezuelas-economy/3323566001/

21. Maxim Lott, How socialism turned Venezuela from the wealthiest country in South America into an economic basket case, Fox News, January 26, 2019, https://www.foxnews.com/world/how-socialism-turned-venezuela-from-the-wealthiest-country-in-south-america-into-an-economic-basket-case

22. Sevil Omer, Venezuela crisis: Facts, FAQs, and how to help, January 12, 2022, https://www.worldvision.org/disaster-relief-news-stories/venezuela-crisis-facts

23. Valerie Strauss and Daniel Southeri, How Many Died? New Evidence Suggests Far Higher Numbers for the Victims of Mao Zedong's Era, Washington Post, July 17, 1994, https://www.washingtonpost.com/archive/politics/1994/07/17/how-many-died-new-evidence-suggests-far-higher-numbers-for-the-victims-of-mao-zedongs-era/01044df5-03dd-49f4-a453-a033c5287bce/

24. Communist Party Congress. How China picks its leaders, BBC, October 7, 2017, https://www.bbc.com/news/world-asia-china-41250273

25. Amnesty International, China 2022, https://www.amnesty.org/en/location/asia-and-the-pacific/east-asia/china/report-china/

26. CBS News, Millions under lockdown as China faces multiple COVID outbreaks ahead of Beijing Winter Olympics, January 12, 2022, https://www.cbsnews.com/news/beijing-winter-olympics-china-covid-omicron-lockdown/

27. Charlie Campbell, "The Entire System is Designed to Suppress Us." What the Chinese Surveillance State Means for the Rest of the World, TIME,

November, 21, 2019, https://time.com/5735411/china-surveillance-privacy-issues/

28.Sylvia Chang & Kelly Ng, Burnt out or jobless – meet China's 'full-time children', BBC, July 17, 2023,
https://www.bbc.com/news/world-asia-china-66172192

29.Margaret Pearson, Meg Rithmire, Kellee S. Tsai, Party-State Capitalism in China, University of California Press Volume 120, Issue 827 September 1, 2021,https://online.ucpress.edu/currenthistory/article/120/827/207/118341/Party-State-Capitalism-in-China

30.Jeff Wallenfeldt, The Rise of Castro and the Outbreak of Revolution, Britannica, https://www.britannica.com/event/Cuban-Revolution/The-rise-of-Castro-and-the-outbreak-of-revolution

31.Bureau of Democracy, Human Rights, and Labor, 2022 Country Reports on Human Rights Practices: Cuba, U.S. Department of State, 2022, https://www.state.gov/reports/2022-country-reports-on-human-rights-practices/cuba/

32.Will Freeman, Why the Situation in Cuba is Deteriorating, Council on Foreign Relations, April 25, 2023,
 https://www.cfr.org/in-brief/why-situation-cuba-deteriorating

33.Encyclopedia Britannica, Russian Revolution, Britannica, August 11, 2023, https://www.britannica.com/event/Russian-Revolution/The-February-Revolution

34.BBC, Joseph Stalin: National hero or cold-blooded murderer? BBC, https://www.bbc.co.uk/teach/joseph-stalin-national-hero-or-cold-blooded-murderer/zhv747h

35.Wikipedia, Human rights in the Soviet Union,
https://en.wikipedia.org/wiki/Human_rights_in_the_Soviet_Union

36.Revelations from the Russian Archives, Library of Congress, https://www.loc.gov/exhibits/archives/intn.html

37.Andrzej Wyszynkski (1949) Teoria dowodow sadowych w prawie radziechkim(PDF) Biblioteka Zrzeszenia Prawnikow Demokratow pp. 153, 162

38.Central Intelligence Agency, Living Standards in the Soviet Union and the United States, April 5, 1985,
 https://www.cia.gov/readingroom/docs/CIA-RDP87M01152R000200130024-5.pdf

39.Will Kenton, Nordic Model: Comparing The Economic System to the U.S., Investopedia, January 27, 2021,
 https://www.investopedia.com/terms/n/nordic-model.asp

40.Lawrence W. Reed, The Dark Side of Paradise: A Brief History of America's Utopian Experiments in Communal Living, FEE Stories, June 13,

2021, https://fee.org/articles/the-dark-side-of-paradise-a-brief-history-of-americas-utopian-experiments-in-communal-living/

41.Garrett Hardin, "The Tragedy of the Commons", Science. 162 (3859): 1243-1248 (1968)

42.William Forster Lloyd, "Two Lectures on the Checks to Population", 1833

CHAPTER THREE

1.Peter J Boettke & Robert L Heilbroner, capitalism, Britannica, August 8, 2023,
https://www.britannica.com/money/topic/capitalism
2.Adam Smith, An Inquiry Into The Nature and Causes of the Wealth of Nations, Books I, II, III, IV, & V, (Meta Libri, 2007),
http://metalibri.incubadora.fapesp.br
3.U.S. Constitution, Amendment X
4.Merriam-Webster, 2003,
 https://www.merriam-webster.com/dictionary/laissez-faire
5.Tyler Halloran, A Brief History of the Corporate Form and Why it Matters, Fordham Journal of Corporate & Financial Law, November 18, 2018,
https://news.law.fordham.edu/jcfl/2018/11/18/a-brief-history-of-the-corporate-form-and-why-it-matters/
6.Maggie Potter, What Was It Like to Run a Business in the 18th Century?, History 1700s, https://www.history1700s.com/index.php/articles/14-guest-authors/2125-what-was-it-like-to-run-a-business-in-the-18th-century.html
7.Professor Gerald Eggert, The Lives of Pre-Industrial Workers, One Minute Essays, Penn State University,
https://www.engr.psu.edu/mtah/essays/workers_lives.htm
8.Joshua J. Mark, Daily Live in Colonial America, World History.org, April 8, 2021, https://www.worldhistory.org/article/1722/daily-life-in-colonial-america/
9.Thomas West, Poverty and Welfare in the American Founding, Heritage.org, May 19, 2015, https://www.heritage.org/poverty-and-inequality/report/poverty-and-welfare-the-american-founding
10.Life for Children in Victorian England, Glad ur not … poor and destitute, https://www.birmingham.gov.uk/info/50139/explore_and_discover/1609/life_for_children_in_victorian_britain/2
11.The President James K. Polk Historic Site, 12031 Lancaster Highway, Pineville, NC 28134, https://www.jameskpolk.net/
12.Morgan Greenwald, Dunkin' Employee Reveals What Happens To All Those Uneaten Donuts At The End Of The Day, In The Know by Yahoo!, July 13, 2022, https://www.intheknow.com/post/dunkin-extra-donuts-food-waste/
13.Laura Hales and Alisha Coleman-Jensen, Food Insecurity for Households with Children Rose in 2020, Disrupting Decade-long Decline, Economic Research Service, U.S. Department of Agriculture, February 7, 2022, https://www.ers.usda.gov/amber-waves/2022/february/food-insecurity-for-households-with-children-rose-in-2020-disrupting-decade-long-decline/

14.State of Homelessness: 2023 Edition, National Alliance to End Homelessness, https://endhomelessness.org/homelessness-in-america/homelessness-statistics/state-of-homelessness/

15.Peter G Peterson Foundation, 7 Key Trends in Poverty in the United States, Peter G Peterson Foundation, February 27, 2023, https://www.pgpf.org/blog/2023/02/7-key-trends-in-poverty-in-the-united-states

16.Testimony of Sharon Parrott, President, The Nation Has Made Progress Against Poverty But Policy Advances Are Needed to Reduce Still-High Hardship, Center on Budget and Policy Priorities, July 28, 2022, https://www.cbpp.org/research/poverty-and-inequality/the-nation-has-made-progress-against-poverty-but-policy-advances

17.Seth Hanlon and Nick Buffle, The Forbes 400 Pay Lower Tax Rates Than Many Ordinary American, American Progress, October 7, 2021, https://www.americanprogress.org/article/forbes-400-pay-lower-tax-rates-many-ordinary-americans/

18.Alexander Abad-Santos, Instead of Raises, McDonald's Tells Workers to Sign Up for Food Stamps, The Atlantic, October 24, 2013, https://www.theatlantic.com/business/archive/2013/10/instead-living-wage-mcdonalds-tells-workers-sign-food-stamps/309625/

19.Hanna Miao, Walmart and McDonald's are among top employers of Medicaid and food stamp beneficiaries, report says, CNBC, November 19, 2020, https://www.cnbc.com/2020/11/19/walmart-and-mcdonalds-among-top-employers-of-medicaid-and-food-stamp-beneficiaries.html

20.David T. Ellwood, The Plight of the Working Poor, Brookings,November 1, 1999, https://www.brookings.edu/articles/the-plight-of-the-working-poor/

21.Center for Poverty & Inequality Research, University of Carolina, Davis, Who are the working poor in America? Data from Bureau of Labor Statistics, https://poverty.ucdavis.edu/faq/who-are-working-poor-america

22.Kerryn Higgs, How the world embraced consumerism, BBC Future, January 20, 2021, https://www.bbc.com/future/article/20210120-how-the-world-became-consumerist

23.The Economist, Big Food Corporations Are Making The World Fat, The Economist, Business Insider, December 21, 2012, https://www.businessinsider.com/big-food-corporations-are-making-the-world-fat-2012-12

24.Nell Boeschenstein, How The Food Industry Manipulates Taste Buds With 'Salt Sugar Fat', NPR Eating and Health, February 26, 2013, https://www.npr.org/sections/thesalt/2013/02/26/172969363/how-the-food-industry-manipulates-taste-buds-with-salt-sugar-fat

25.Karl Marx & Frederick Engels, Manifesto of the Communist Party, Moscow, 1848, Marxist Internet Archive (marxists.org) 1987, 2000, 2010. Creative Commons Attribution-Share-Alike License (Page 46)

26.Stephanie Pappas, The toll of Job Loss, American Psychological Association, October 1, 2020, https://www.apa.org/monitor/2020/10/toll-job-loss

27.Abraham Lincoln, The Gettysburg Address, November 19, 1863

28.Rakesh Kochhar and Stella Sechopoulos, How the American middle class has changed in the past five decades, Pew Research Center, April 20, 2022, https://www.pewresearch.org/short-reads/2022/04/20/how-the-american-middle-class-has-changed-in-the-past-five-decades/

29.Drew DeSilver, For most U.S. workers, real wages have barely budged in decades, Pew Research Center, August 7, 2018, https://www.pewresearch.org/short-reads/2018/08/07/for-most-us-workers-real-wages-have-barely-budged-for-decades/

30.Census Bureau, For Immediate Release: February 24, 2022, Census Bureau Releases New Educational Attainment Data, Census.gov, February 24, 2022, https://www.census.gov/newsroom/press-releases/2022/educational-attainment.html

31.Lawrence Mishel, Elise Gould, and Josh Bivens, Wage Stagnation in Nine Charts, Economic Policy Institute, January 6, 2015, https://www.epi.org/publication/charting-wage-stagnation/

32.John Schmitt, Elise Gould, and Josh Bivens, America's Slow-Motion Wage Crisis, Economic Policy Institute, September 13, 2018, https://www.epi.org/publication/americas-slow-motion-wage-crisis-four-decades-of-slow-and-unequal-growth-2/

33.Aimee Picchi, Most middle-class American say they can't support their cost of living, survey finds, CBS News Money Watch, July 20, 2022, https://www.cbsnews.com/news/inflation-75-percent-of-middle-class-americans-say-income-below-cost-of-living/

34.Juhohn Lee, Why American wages haven't grown despite increases in productivity, CNBC, July 19, 2022, https://www.cnbc.com/2022/07/19/heres-how-labor-dynamism-affects-wage-growth-in-america.html

35.Varsha Adibhatla, Advertising & Over-consumption, Medium, July 4, 2017, https://medium.com/@varsha.ravindranath/advertising-over-consumption-584fbf721115

36.Will Kenton, What Is Planned Obsolescence? How Strategy Works and Example, Investopedia, December 27, 2022, https://www.investopedia.com/terms/p/planned_obsolescence.asp

37.Theo Wayt, Auto giants like BMW, GM and Toyota make drivers 'subscribe' for basic features, NY Post, August 21, 2022,

https://nypost.com/2022/08/21/auto-giants-like-bmw-gm-and-toyota-make-drivers-subscribe-for-basic-features/
38.Aaron Garcia, Does Medicare Cover CPAP Machines? GoHealth, https://www.gohealth.com/medicare/coverages-benefits/cpap-machines/
39.Reema Khrais and Anais Amin, Did department stores train people to be difficult customers?, MarketPlace, August 13, 2021, https://www.marketplace.org/2021/08/13/did-department-stores-train-people-to-be-difficult-customers/
40.Bridget McCrea, Is The Customer Really Always Right?, TED Magazine, January 17, 2019, https://tedmag.com/is-the-customer-really-always-right/
41.Nathan Miller, (1992), Theodore Roosevelt, A Life, pp. 459-460, William Morrow & Co.
42.Micky Z, 50 American Revolutions You Are Not Supposed To Know, The Disinformation Company, 2005, New York, p. 87
43.Congress Acts on Traffic and Auto Safety, CQ Almanac, Congressional Quarterly, 1966, Retrieved April 27, 2016, pp 266-268
44.Molly Niesen, The Little Old Lady Has Teeth: The U.S. Federal Trade Commission and the Advertising Industry, Advertising & Society Review, 1970-1973, Retrieved July 19, 2012
45.The New York Times, Nader Forms Unit to Seek Donations, The New York Times, June 2, 1971
46.David E. McCraw, The Freedom from Information Act: A Look Back at Nader, FOIA, & What Went Wrong, Yale Law Journal, Retrieved September 20, 2023, www.yalelawjournal.org
47.Michael Kelly, Celebrating THE Clean Water Champion, Clean Water Action, Retrieved September 20, 2023
48.Staff, W.N.N., An Unheard of Dream: Ralph Nader's 50 Years in Whistleblowing, Whistleblower Network News, Retrieved September 20, 2023
49.PBS Newshour Classroom, How Ralph Nader defined consumer rights, PBS Newshour Classroom, Retrieved September 20, 2023

CHAPTER FOUR

1.Rebecca Beatrice Brooks, The Industrial Revolution in America, History of Massachusetts Blog, April 11, 2018,
 https://historyofmassachusetts.org/industrial-revolution-america/
2.National Geographic, Industrialization, Labor, and Life, National Geographic,
https://education.nationalgeographic.org/resource/industrialization-labor-and-life/
3.Library of Congress, The Industrial Revolution in the United States, Library of Congress Archives,
 https://www.loc.gov/classroom-materials/industrial-revolution-in-the-united-states/
4.Industrial Revolution Working Conditions: What Were They Like? History on the Net 2000-2003, Salem Media, August 30, 2003,
https://www.historyonthenet.com/industrial-revolution-working-conditions
5.Teach Democracy, BRIA 23 1 b Progressives and the Era of Trustbusting, CONSTITUTIONAL RIGHTS FOUNDATION, Bill of Rights in Action, Volume 23, No. 1, Spring 2007, https://www.crf-usa.org/bill-of-rights-in-action/bria-23-1-b-progressives-and-the-era-of-trustbusting.html
6.Andrew Beattie, A History of U.S. Monopolies, Investopedia, September 11, 2022,
 https://www.investopedia.com/insights/history-of-us-monopolies/
7.Stacy Mitchell and Susan R. Holmberg, America's Monopoly Problem: Why It Matters and What We Can Do About It, Institute For Local Self-Reliance, July 2020, https://ilsr.org/fighting-monopoly-power/americas-monopoly-problem-and-why-it-matters/
8.APA, Rousseau, J. –j. (2004). The Social Contract, Penguin Books
9.Andrea Britton, Freedom in the absolute: a self-destructive Paradox, Medium, May 18 2022,
 https://medium.com/@mediaboy441/freedom-in-the-absolute-a-self-destructive-paradox-eac6b492738b
10.Dr. Michael Arnheim, Continuity and Change after the Fall of the Roman Empire, World History Encyclopedia,July 4, 2022,
https://www.worldhistory.org/article/2027/continuity-and-change-after-the-fall-of-the-roman/
11.Marcus Magister, The Fall of Rome and its Effects on Post-Roman and Medieval Europe, Medium.com, January 28, 2017,
https://medium.com/@marcusmagister/the-fall-of-rome-and-its-effects-on-post-roman-and-medieval-europe-11a888a98102
12.Sherman Anti-Trust Act, (1890), National Archives,
https://www.archives.gov/milestone-documents/sherman-anti-trust-act

13.Daniel Ruddy, (2016), Theodore the Great: Conservative Crusader, Washington DC, Regnery History

14.White House Historical Association, Biography for President Roosevelt, Theodore Roosevelt,
 https://www.whitehouse.gov/about-the-white-house/presidents/theodore-roosevelt/

15.Nathan Miller, (1992), Theodore Roosevelt, A Life, pp. 459-460, William Morrow & Co.

16.Troy Segal, Clayton Antitrust Act of 1914: History, Amendments, Significance, April 18, 2023,
 https://www.investopedia.com/terms/c/clayton-antitrust-act.asp

17.U-S-History.com, Roaring Twenties, October 31, 2018, U-S-History.com Online Highways, http://u-s-history.com/pages

18.Office of the Historian, The Immigration Act of 1924 (The Johnson-Reed Act), History.State.Gov, https://history.state.gov/milestones/1921-1936/immigration-act

19.Federal Reserve Bank of St. Louis, What Caused the Great Depression?, Federal Reserve Bank of St. Louis, https://www.stlouisfed.org/the-great-depression/curriculum/economic-episodes-in-american-history-part-5

20.Dan Bryan, 'The 1933 Banking Crisis – from Detroit's Collapse to Roosevelt's Bank Holiday, American History USA, Retrieved December 5, 2014

21.William Silber, 'Why Did FDR's Bank Holiday Succeed?' Federal Reserve Bank of New York Economic Policy Review pp 19-30, Retrieved February 22, 2020

22.William Leuchtenburg, 'Professor Emeritus of History University of North Carolina', (October, 4, 2016), Retrieved March 3, 2021

23.Julia Maues, Banking Act of 1933 (Glass-Steagall), Federal Reserve History, November 22, 2013,
 https://www.federalreservehistory.org/essays/glass-steagall-act

24.Will Kenton, Securities Act of 1933: Significance and History, Investopedia, October 20, 2020,
 https://www.investopedia.com/terms/s/securitiesact1933.asp

25.National Labor Relations Board, National Labor Relations Act, https://www.nlrb.gov/guidance/key-reference-materials/national-labor-relations-act

26.Encyclopedia Britannica, Combinations Acts, https://www.britannica.com/money/topic/Combination-Acts

27.Eric Arnesen, Encyclopedia of U.S. Labor and Working-Class, (2007,Vol 1, New York, Routledge), p 1540

28.History 1930, Social Security Administration, Retrieved May 21, 2009, https://www.ssa.gov/history/1930.html

29.Social Security, Pre Social Security Period,
https://www.ssa.gov/history/briefhistory3.html
30.Pub. L. 75-718, ch. 676, 52 Stat 1060, June 25, 1938
31.WHD U.S. Wage and Hour Division, The Fair Labor Standards Act of
1938, As Amended, U.S. Department of Labor, Wage and Hour Division,
WH Publication 1318, Revised May 2011,
https://www.dol.gov/sites/dolgov/files/WHD/legacy/files/FairLaborStand
Act.pdf
32.Marguerite Ward, A brief history of the 8-hour workday, which changed
how Americans work, CNBC, May 3, 2017,
 https://www.cnbc.com/2017/05/03/how-the-8-hour-workday-changed-
how-americans-work.html
33.John R Commons and Associates, History of Labour in the United States,
[1896-1932], 4 vol. 1921-1957, p viii
34.Christopher L. Tomlins, The state and the unions: labor relations, law, and
the organized labor movement in America. 1880-1960, (1985) pp 112 & 133
35.Ronni Sandroff, The History of Unions in the United States,Investopedia,
September 1, 2022,
 https://www.investopedia.com/financial-edge/0113/the-history-of-unions-
in-the-united-states.aspx
36.G. William Domhoff, Who Rules America?, University of California at
Santa Cruz, February 2013,
https://whorulesamerica.ucsc.edu/power/history_of_labor_unions.html
37.Wendy Connett, Are Labor Unions Effective?, Investopedia, February 26,
2023, https://www.investopedia.com/financial-edge/0113/are-labor-unions-
effective.aspx
38.Thomas I. Palley, The Forces Making for an Economic Collapse: Why a
depression could happen, The Atlantic Monthly, July 1996, Volume 278, No.
1, pages 44-58,
 https://www.theatlantic.com/magazine/archive/1996/07/the-forces-
making-for-an-economic-collapse/376621/
39.Shmoop University, Economy in the 1950s, Schmoop, 2017,
https://www.shmoop.com/1950s/economy.html%3E
40.Shmoop University, Economy in the 1960s, Schmoop, 2017,
https://www.shmoop.com/1960s/economy.html1
41.Chart Of The Day, Dow Jones Chart since 1900 (Inflation-Adjusted),
Retrieved October 6, 2023,
 https://www.chartoftheday.com/dow-jones-chart-since-1900-inflation-
adjusted
42.FRED, St. Louis Federal Reserve, GDP Gross Domestic Product (1945-
Present), FRED, Retrieve October 6, 2023,
https://fred.stlouisfed.org/series/GDP

43.Our World In Data, Productivity: output per hour worked (adjusted for inflation-1950-2019), Our World in Data, Retrieved October 6, 2023, https://ourworldindata.org/grapher/labor-productivity-per-hour-PennWorldTable?tab=chart&country=~USA

44.Lawrence Mishel, Elise Gould, and Josh Bivens, Wage Stagnation in Nine Charts, Economic Policy Institute, January 6, 2015, https://www.epi.org/publication/charting-wage-stagnation/

45.John Schmitt, Elise Gould, and Josh Bivens, America's Slow-Motion Wage Crisis, Economic Policy Institute, September 13, 2018, https://www.epi.org/publication/americas-slow-motion-wage-crisis-four-decades-of-slow-and-unequal-growth-2/

46.FRED, St. Louis Federal Reserve, Unemployment Rate (1948-2023), FRED, Retrieved October 6, 2023, https://fred.stlouisfed.org/series/UNRATE

47.FRED, St. Louis Federal Reserve, Median Household Income (Adjusted for Inflation, 1984-2022), FRED, Retrieved October 6, 2023, https://fred.stlouisfed.org/series/MEHOINUSA672N

48.Statista, Educational attainment distribution in the United States from 1960 to 2021, Statista, Retrieved October 6, 2023, https://www.statista.com/statistics/184260/educational-attainment-in-the-us/

49.TED: The Economics Daily, Working wives in married-couple families, 1967-2011, U.S. Bureau of Labor Statistics, June 2, 2014, https://www.bls.gov/opub/ted/2014/ted_20140602.htm

50.Melanie Hanson, Average Cost of College by Year (Adjusted for Inflation-1969-2020), Education Data Initiative, January 9, 2022 , https://educationdata.org/average-cost-of-college-by-year

51.FRED, St. Louis Federal Reserve, Median Sales Price of House Sold in the United States (1963-2023), FRED, Retrieved October 6, 2023, https://fred.stlouisfed.org/series/MSPUS

52.Tim Henderson, Investors Bought a Quarter of Homes Sold Last Year, Driving Up Rents, Stateline, July 22, 2022, https://stateline.org/2022/07/22/investors-bought-a-quarter-of-homes-sold-last-year-driving-up-rents/

53.FRED, St. Louis Federal Reserve, Highest Individual Income Tax Brackets (1913-2018), FRED, Retrieved October 6, 2023, https://fred.stlouisfed.org/series/IITTRHB

54.Treasury.gov Fiscal Data, What is the national debt?, Retrieved October 6, 2023, https://fiscaldata.treasury.gov/americas-finance-guide/national-debt/

55.David Schaper, Potholes, Grid Failures, Aging Tunnels And Bridges: Infrastructure Gets A C-Minus, NPR, March 3, 2021, https://www.npr.org/2021/03/03/973054080/potholes-grid-failures-aging-tunnels-and-bridges-nations-infrastructure-gets-a-c

56.Chris Versace, Lenore Elle Hawkins, Mark Abssy, Just How Bad is America's Infrastructure and How Can Investors Benefit from the New Infrastructure Bill?, Nasdaq Articles, November 17, 2021, https://www.nasdaq.com/articles/just-how-bad-is-americas-infrastructure-and-how-can-investors-benefit-from-the-new

57.J. Creamer, EA Shrider, K Burns, F. Chen, What is the current poverty rate in the United States?, Center for Poverty & Inequality, University of California, Davis, September 2022, Data from US Census Bureau October 2022, https://poverty.ucdavis.edu/faq/what-current-poverty-rate-united-states

CHAPTER FIVE

1.Barry Nielsen, Stagnation in the 1970s, Investopedia, August 18, 2023, https://www.investopedia.com/articles/economics/08/1970-stagflation.asp

2.Owen Rust, The Economic Effects of the Vietnam War, The Collector, October 7, 2023, https://www.thecollector.com/vietnam-war-economic-effects/

3.J. Creamer, EA Shrider, K Burns, F. Chen, What is the current poverty rate in the United States?, Center for Poverty & Inequality, University of California, Davis, September 2022, Data from US Census Bureau October 2022,
 https://poverty.ucdavis.edu/faq/what-current-poverty-rate-united-states

4.History.com editors, The Great Society, History.com, November 17, 2017, https://www.history.com/topics/1960s/great-society

5.James Chen, Bretton Woods Agreement and the Institutions It Created Explained, Investopedia, March 21, 2022,
https://www.investopedia.com/terms/b/brettonwoodsagreement.asp

6.Dominic Diongson, What Was the Bretton Woods System? How Did It End?, The Street, November7, 2022,
 https://www.thestreet.com/dictionary/b/bretton-woods-system

7.Will Kenton, What Is Nixon Shock? Definition, What Happened, and Aftereffects, Investopedia, August 30, 2022,
https://www.investopedia.com/terms/n/nixon-shock.asp

8.Office of the Historian, Oil Embargo, 1973-1974, U.S. State Department, https://history.state.gov/milestones/1969-1976/oil-embargo

9.Laurel Graefe, Oil Shock, 1978-79, Federal Reserve Bank of Atlanta, Federal Reserve History, Retrieved October 11, 2023,
https://www.federalreservehistory.org/essays/oil-shock-of-1978-79

10.Chart Of The Day, Dow Jones Chart since 1900 (Inflation-Adjusted), Retrieved October 6, 2023,
 https://www.chartoftheday.com/dow-jones-chart-since-1900-inflation-adjusted

11.FRED, St. Louis Federal Reserve, Unemployment Rate (1948-2023), FRED, Retrieved October 6, 2023,
 https://fred.stlouisfed.org/series/UNRATE

12.J. Creamer, EA Shrider, K Burns, F. Chen, What is the current poverty rate in the United States?, Center for Poverty & Inequality, University of California, Davis, September 2022, Data from US Census Bureau October 2022, https://poverty.ucdavis.edu/faq/what-current-poverty-rate-united-states

13.FRED, St. Louis Federal Reserve, Federal Reserve Effective Interest Rate (1954-2021), FRED, Retrieved October 6, 2023, https://fred.stlouisfed.org/series/FEDFUNDS

14.Emily Peck, Real incomes fell last year. No wonder Americans were bummed out, AXIOS, Retrieved October 11, 2023, https://www.axios.com/2023/09/12/real-incomes-fell-last-year-no-wonder-americans-were-bummed-out

15.MACROTRENDS, U.S. Inflation Rate 1960-2023, Macro Trends, Retrieved October 11, 2023, https://www.macrotrends.net/countries/USA/united-states/inflation-rate-cpi

16.Will Kenton, Reagonomics: Definition, Policies, and Impact, Investopedia, January 10, 2023, https://www.investopedia.com/terms/r/reaganomics.asp

17.CFI Team, Reaganomics, CFI, Retrieved October 13, 2023, https://corporatefinanceinstitute.com/resources/economics/reaganomics/

18.Liz Manning, Neoliberalism: What It Is, With Examples and Pros and Cons, Investopedia, Retrieved October 13, 2023, https://www.investopedia.com/terms/n/neoliberalism.asp

19.David R. Harper, Supply-Side Economics: What You Need to Know, Investopedia, Retrieved October 13, 2023, https://www.investopedia.com/articles/05/011805.asp

20.Mary Hall, Demand-Side Economics Definition, Examples of Policies, Investopedia, August 24, 2023, https://www.investopedia.com/ask/answers/040915/what-demandside-economics.asp

21.Sky News, Amazon, Apple, Facebook and Google 'are monopolies', warns Congress report, Sky News, October 7, 2020, https://news.sky.com/story/amazon-apple-facebook-and-google-are-monopolies-warns-congress-report-12098254

22.Liz Manning, Neoliberalism: What It Is, With Examples and Pros and Cons, Investopedia, July 20, 2022, https://www.investopedia.com/terms/n/neoliberalism.asp

23.Stephen Maher, Jack Welch Is Dead. Neoliberalism Lives On., Jacobin, 3/6/2020, https://jacobin.com/2020/03/jack-welch-general-electric-shareholder-obituary

24.Michael Moore, Roger & Me, film, 1989

25.Steven Dandaneau, A Town Abandoned: Flint, Michigan Confronts Deindustrialization, SUNY Press, pp. 21

26.Melissa Burden and Michael Wayland, GM to invest $877M in Flint truck plant, The Detroit News, August 4, 2015

27.Financial Transparency Coalition, Farming for Rats: Perverse Incentives and Illicit Financial Flows, Financial Transparency Coalition, March 28, 2013, https://financialtransparency.org/farming-for-rats-perverse-incentives-and-illicit-financial-flows/

28.James Chen, Nash Equilibrium: How It Works in Game Theory, Examples, Plus Prisoner's Dilemma, Investopedia, April 24, 2023, https://www.investopedia.com/terms/n/nash-equilibrium.asp

29.George Monbiot, Neoliberalism – the ideology at the root of all our problems, The Guardian, April 15, 2016, https://www.theguardian.com/books/2016/apr/15/neoliberalism-ideology-problem-george-monbiot

30.Stephen Metcalf, Neoliberalism: the idea that swallowed the world, The Guardian, August 18, 2017, https://www.theguardian.com/news/2017/aug/18/neoliberalism-the-idea-that-changed-the-world

31.Brianna Scott, Jeanette Woods, Alisa Chang, How AI could perpetuate racism, sexism and other biases in society, NPR All Things Considered, July 19, 2023, https://www.npr.org/2023/07/19/1188739764/how-ai-could-perpetuate-racism-sexism-and-other-biases-in-society

32.Milton Friedman, Capitalism And Freedom, The University of Chicago Press, Chicago and London, Reprinted 2002, (1962)

33.John Uri, 60 Years Ago: NASA Launches its First Satellite, NASA, October 10, 2018, https://www.nasa.gov/history/60-years-ago-nasa-launches-its-first-satellite/

34.Science Museum, From ARPANET To The Internet, Science Museum, November 2, 2012, https://www.sciencemuseum.org.uk/objects-and-stories/arpanet-internet

35.Zachary A. Goldfarb, Michelle Boorstein, Pope Francis denounces 'trickle-down' economic theories in sharp criticism of inequality, The Washington Post, November 26, 2013, Retrieved April 6, 2018

CHAPTER SIX

1.Mark J. Perry, Let's Not Forget the Decade the Liberals Love to Hate: The 1960s and President Kennedy's Successful, Supply-side Tax Cuts, AEI, August 17, 2013, https://www.aei.org/carpe-diem/lets-not-forget-the-decade-the-liberals-love-to-hate-the-1960s-and-president-kennedys-successful-supply-side-tax-cuts/
2.Daniel J. Mitchell, The 1950s Economic Golden Age Is a Myth: High marginal tax rates in the 1950s failed to generate revenue and stunted economic performance., International Liberty, November 15, 2017, https://fee.org/articles/the-1950s-economic-golden-age-is-a-myth/
3.Adam Hayes, Julie Bang, Laffer Curve: History and Critique, Investopedia, February 16, 2023,
https://www.investopedia.com/terms/l/laffercurve.asp
4.David Frum, How We Got Here: The 70s, 2000, New York, Basic Books, p. 293
5.James N. Giglio, The Presidency of John F. Kennedy (2nd edition), 2006, University Press of Kansas, p. 99
6.USDA, A Short History of SNAP, USDA Food and Nutrition Service, Retrieved October 19 ,2023,
 https://www.fns.usda.gov/snap/short-history-snap
7.History.COM Editors, The Great Society, History.com, November 17, 2017, Updated August 28, 2018,
 https://www.history.com/topics/1960s/great-society
8.J. Creamer, EA Shrider, K Burns, F. Chen, What is the current poverty rate in the United States?, Center for Poverty & Inequality, University of California, Davis, September 2022, Data from US Census Bureau October 2022,
 https://poverty.ucdavis.edu/faq/what-current-poverty-rate-united-states
9.Branka Vuleta, When Was Welfare Created in the US?, LegalJobs, October 25, 2022, https://legaljobs.io/blog/when-was-welfare-created/
10.Ronald H. Spector, Vietnam War 1954-1975, Britannica, September 30, 2023, https://www.britannica.com/event/Vietnam-War/The-United-States-negotiates-a-withdrawal
11.Owen Rust, The Economic Effects of the Vietnam War, The Collector, October 7, 2023, https://www.thecollector.com/vietnam-war-economic-effects/
12.Will Kenton, What Is Nixon Shock? Definition, What Happened, and Aftereffects, Investopedia, August 30, 2022,
 https://www.investopedia.com/terms/n/nixon-shock.asp
13.Simone McCarthy, Fifty years after Nixon's historic visit to China, questions hang over the US-China future, CNN, February 21, 2022,

https://www.cnn.com/2022/02/21/china/nixon-mao-china-50th-anniversary-intl-hnk-mic/index.html

14.The Editors of Encyclopedia Britannica, War on Drugs, Encyclopedia Britannica, August 22, 2023,
 https://www.britannica.com/topic/war-on-drugs

15.Barry Nielsen, Stagnation in the 1970s, Investopedia, August 18, 2023, https://www.investopedia.com/articles/economics/08/1970-stagflation.asp

16.FRED, St. Louis Federal Reserve, Federal Reserve Effective Interest Rate (1954-2021), FRED, Retrieved October 6, 2023,
https://fred.stlouisfed.org/series/FEDFUNDS

17.Office of the Historian, Oil Embargo, 1973-1974, U.S. State Department, https://history.state.gov/milestones/1969-1976/oil-embargo

18.Fred Frommer, How Gerald Ford Tried to Fight Inflation, Ford's 'Whip Inflation Now (WIN)' effort tried to tamp down inflation with a collective, can-do approach. It didn't work out. ,History.com,September 21, 2022,
 https://www.history.com/news/ford-inflation-win-program

19.The Editors of Encyclopedia Britannica, Jimmy Carter, Britannica, October 5, 2023,
 https://www.britannica.com/biography/Jimmy-Carter

20.Federal Reserve History, Oil Shock of 1978-79, Federal Reserve History, Retrieved October 19, 2023,
 https://www.federalreservehistory.org/essays/oil-shock-of-1978-79

21.Harold Relyea, Thomas Carr, The executive branch, creation and reorganization, (2003), Nova Publishers, p. 29

22.Gerhard Peters, John T Woolley, Department of Education Organization Act Statement on Signing S. 210 Into Law, (October 17, 1979), The American Presidency Project

23.Jimmy Carter, Keeping Faith, Memoirs of a President, Bantam Books, (1982), pp. 86-87

24.James R. Cannon, Franklin D Richey, Practical Implications in Business Aviation Management, (2012), Government Institutes

25.PBS, The Georgia Mafia, Jimmy Carter, WBGH American Experience, February 17, 2017, Retrieved March 13, 2017

26.The Editors of Encyclopedia Britannica, Ronald Reagan, Britannica, September 28, 2023,
 https://www.britannica.com/biography/Ronald-Reagan/Presidency

27.Will Kenton, Reagonomics: Definition, Policies, and Impact, Investopedia, January 10, 2023,
 https://www.investopedia.com/terms/r/reaganomics.asp

28.Joseph Thorndike, Reagan's Tax Cut Just Turned 40 — And It's Still The Most Important Tax Reform Since World War II, Forbes, September 3, 2021, https://www.forbes.com/sites/taxnotes/2021/09/03/reagans-tax-cut-just-turned-40---and-its-still-the-most-important-tax-reform-since-world-war-ii

29.   David Wessel, How Reagan's Tax Cuts Fared, NPR, December 8, 2017,
 https://www.npr.org/2017/12/08/569345901/how-reagans-tax-cuts-fared

30.CBO, Historical Budget Data, Retrieved May 28, 2019

31.Union of Concerned Scientists, A Brief History of US Fuel Efficiency Standards, Where we are—and where are we going?, Union of Concerned Scientists, July 25, 2006, Updated December 6, 2017,
 https://www.ucsusa.org/resources/brief-history-us-fuel-efficiency

32.Olivia Campbell, Here's what happened when Reagan went after healthcare programs. It's not good. The latest cuts have a less-than-stellar precedent, Medium, September 13, 2017,
 https://timeline.com/reagan-trump-healthcare-cuts-8cf64aa242eb

33.Matt Ford, Cook County Jail, America's Largest Mental Hospital is a Jail, The Atlantic, Retrieved September 13, 2015

34.Ron Dicker, John Oliver Explains How Ronald Reagan 'Turbocharged' Homelessness, Huffington Post, November 1, 2021,
 https://www.huffpost.com/entry/john-oliver-homelessness_n_617feda6e4b03072d7069502

35.David Pirtle, James Greene, Kathy Sibert, Why Some Homeless Choose The Streets Over Shelters, NPR Talk of the Nation, December 6, 2012,
 https://www.npr.org/2012/12/06/166666265/why-some-homeless-choose-the-streets-over-shelters

36.Audrey Jensen, Jill Ryan, Chloe Jones, Madeline Ackley, Two cities tried to fix homelessness, only one succeeded, Cronkite News, December 14, 2020,
 https://cronkitenews.azpbs.org/howardcenter/caring-for-covid-homeless/stories/homeless-funding-housing-first.html

37.LA Times Archives, Education Dept. Won't Be Abolished : Reagan Backs Down, Citing Little Support for Killing Agency, Los Angeles Times, January 29, 1985,
https://www.latimes.com/archives/la-xpm-1985-01-29-mn-13948-story.html

38.Jon Schwarz, THE ORIGIN OF STUDENT DEBT: REAGAN ADVISER WARNED FREE COLLEGE WOULD CREATE A DANGEROUS "EDUCATED PROLETARIAT", The Intercept, August 25, 2022,
 https://theintercept.com/2022/08/25/student-loans-debt-reagan/

39.Thom Hartman, Student Loan Debt Is an American Malignancy Born of Ronald Reagan, Common Dreams, August 26, 2022,
 https://www.commondreams.org/views/2022/08/26/student-loan-debt-american-malignancy-born-ronald-reagan

40.Airline Deregulation Act, Pub L 95-904 49 USC 1371 Approved October, 1978

41.William Black, The Best Way to Rob a Bank is to Own One, Austin University of Texas Press (2005)

42.John Robert Greene, The Presidency of George Bush (2nd Ed) University Press of Kansas, 2015

43.Joseph Pechman, IRS Revenue Procedures, Federal Tax Policy, Joint Committee on Taxation, Summary of Conference Agreement on the Jobs and Growth Tax Relief Reconciliation Act of 2003, May 22, 2003.

44.Duke University, NAFTA, Archived April 20, 2008, Retrieved July 30, 2018,
http://www.law.duke.edu/lib/researchguides/nafta.html

45.Steve Lohr, Accepting the Harsh Truth of a Blue-Collar Recession, The New York Times, December 25, 1991, Retrieved January 5, 2022

46.Jennifer Agiesta, Approval Highs and Lows, Archived, The Wayback Machine, The Washington Post, July 24, 2007

47.The New York Times, The 1992 Campaign: On the Trail, Poll Gives Perot a Clear Lead, The New York Times, June 11, 1992

48.U.S. Customs and Border Protection, North American Free Trade Agreement, June 23, 2023, https://www.cbp.gov/trade/north-american-free-trade-agreement

49.PBS Frontline, Interview with Robert Reich, Former Secretary of Labor, https://www.pbs.org/wgbh/pages/frontline/shows/clinton/interviews/reich2.html

50.Pollwatcher, Robert Reich on NAFTA: I Don't Think It Was A Mistake, Daily KOS, March 30, 2016,
https://www.dailykos.com/stories/2016/3/30/1507138/-Robert-Reich-On-NAFTA-I-Don-t-Think-It-Was-A-Mistake

51.Robert Reich, Robert Reich explains why he helped start EPI in 1986, Economic Policy Institute, Retrieved October 24, 2023,
https://www.epi.org/action/robert-reich-when-i-helped-start-epi-in-1986/

52.On The Issues, Robert Reich on Free Trade, On The Issues, Retrieved October 24, 2023,
https://www.ontheissues.org/celeb/Robert_Reich_Free_Trade.htm

53.Robert Reich, Hillary and Barack, Afta Nafta, Robert Reich.org, February 29, 2008, https://robertreich.org/post/257309371

54.Will Kenton, What Is the North American Free Trade Agreement (NAFTA)?, Investopedia, April 29, 2023,
https://www.investopedia.com/terms/n/nafta.asp

55.Robert Reich, Robert Reich: Trade agreements are simply ravaging the middle class, Salon.com, March 16, 2016, https://www.salon.com/2016/03/16/robert_reich_trade_deals_are_gutting_the_middle_class_partner/

56.Carlos Salas, Bruce Campbell, Robert E. Scott, NAFTA at Seven, EPI, March 21, 2001,
 https://www.epi.org/publication/briefingpapers_nafta01_index/

57.Scott Nevil, What Is a Tariff and Why Are They Important?, Investopedia, May 28, 2023,
 https://www.investopedia.com/terms/t/tariff.asp

58.Robert Whaples, Where Is There Consensus Among American Economic Historians? The Results of a Survey on Forty Positions, The Journal of Economic History, Cambridge University Press, March 1995

59.Peter B Levy, Encyclopedia of the Clinton Presidency, Greenwood Publishing Group, p.57

60.Paul Starr, What Happened to Health Care Reform?, Princeton University, The American Prospect no.20 (Winter 1995: 20-31,
https://www.princeton.edu/~starr/20starr.html

61.Lena Borrelli, What Is The Affordable Care Act (Obamacare)?, Forbes, October 6, 2023, https://www.forbes.com/advisor/health-insurance/what-is-obamacare/

62.Joshua W. Axene, Take a number: Would long wait times in US healthcare be acceptable?, State of Reform, May 30, 2019,
https://stateofreform.com/news/2019/05/take-a-number-would-long-wait-times-in-us-healthcare-be-acceptable/

63."Fiscal 1993 Stimulus Bill Killed." In CQ Almanac 1993, 49th ed., 706-9. Washington, DC: Congressional Quarterly, 1994.
http://library.cqpress.com/cqalmanac/cqal93-1105049.

64.United States Department of Labor, Fact Sheet #28: The Family and Medical Leave Act, Department of Labor Wage and Hour Division, Revised February 2023,
 https://www.dol.gov/agencies/whd/fact-sheets/28-fmla

65.Nick Bryant, How history will judge Bill Clinton, BBC News, Retrieved March 24, 2011, January 15, 2001

66.Steve Schifferes, Bill Clinton's economic legacy, BBC News, Retrieved March 24, 2011, January 15, 2001

67.H. Sultz, K. Young, Health Care USA Understanding its Organization and Delivery, pg. 257

68.Jackie Tortora, Where Did All Our Pensions Go?, AFL-CIO, October 7, 2012, https://aflcio.org/2012/10/7/where-did-all-our-pensions-go

69.Congressional Quarterly, Congress and the Nation, Vol 10 1997-2001 (2002), pp 130-140

70.Mary Pilon, How Bill Clinton's Welfare Reform Changed America, History.com, April 26, 2018, https://www.history.com/news/clinton-1990s-welfare-reform-facts

CHAPTER SEVEN

1.Emily Horton, The Legacy of the 2001 and 2003 "Bush" Tax Cuts, Center on Budget and Policy Priorities, October 23, 2017, https://www.cbpp.org/research/the-legacy-of-the-2001-and-2003-bush-tax-cuts

2.Mike Sylvester, Debt Nation, post two, Small Business Services CPA Group, October 13, 2008, Retrieved November 20, 2019

3.Danielle Kurtzleben, What Did the Iraq War Cost? More Than You Think., US News.com, December 15, 2011, https://www.usnews.com/news/articles/2011/12/15/what-did-the-iraq-war-cost-more-than-you-think

4.Jean Edward Smith, Bush, Simon & Schuster, 2016

5.Jan C. Greenburg, Supreme Conflict: The Inside Story of the Struggle for Control of the United States Supreme Court, New York, Penguin, 2007

6.Sam Dillon, President Signs Landmark No Child Left Behind Education Bill, White House, January 8, 2002

7.The New York Times, Bush Vetoes Child Health Bill Privately, The New York Times, October 4, 2007

8.Robert Draper, Dead Certain: The Presidency of George W. Bush, Free Press, 2007, pp. 295-296

9.Komaron McNair, 56% of Americans say they're not on track to comfortably retire—how to catch up, CNBC, September 8, 2023, https://www.cnbc.com/2023/09/08/56percent-of-americans-say-theyre-not-on-track-to-comfortably-retire.html

10.Michael J. Boyle, 2008 Recession: What It Was and What Caused It, Investopedia, April 30, 2023, https://www.investopedia.com/terms/g/great-recession.asp

11.Wayne Duggan, A Short History Of The Great Recession, Forbes.com, June 21, 2023, https://www.forbes.com/advisor/investing/great-recession/

12.Adam Hayes, American Recovery and Reinvestment Act (ARRA): Objectives and FAQS, Investopedia, June 25, 2023, https://www.investopedia.com/terms/a/american-recovery-and-reinvestment-act.asp

13.Noam N. Levey, Obama signs into law expansion of SCHIP health care program for Children, Chicago Tribune, February 5, 2009, Archived April 30, 2009, Retrieved June 15, 2009

14.CNN, Obama signs tax deal into law, CNN, December 17, 2010, Retrieved December 17, 2010

15.David M. Herszenhorn, Sheryl Gay Stolberg, Democrats Skeptical of Obama on New Tax Plan, The New York Times, December 7, 2010

16.Peter Grier, Health care reform bill 101: Who will pay for reform?, Christian Science Monitor, March 21, 2010, Archived July 6, 2015

17.Jasmine Payne-Patterson, Maye A. Adewale, A history of the federal minimum wage, Economic Policy Institute, August 31, 2023, https://www.epi.org/blog/a-history-of-the-federal-minimum-wage-85-years-later-the-minimum-wage-is-far-from-equitable/

18.Adam Hayes, Dodd-Frank Act: What It Does, Major Components, and Criticisms, Investopedia, August 2, 2023, https://www.investopedia.com/terms/d/dodd-frank-financial-regulatory-reform-bill.asp

19.Will Kenton, Trans-Pacific Partnership: Meaning, Overview, Alternatives, Investopedia, September 10, 2022, https://www.investopedia.com/terms/t/transpacific-partnership-tpp.asp

20.Christopher S. Rugaber, Study: Obama tax hikes on rich didn't hurt economy, or rich, AP News, November 3, 2016, https://apnews.com/article/87553d69f3294e1fb3d0a5912f2e6e31

21.Jonathan Oberlander, Long Time Coming: Why Health Reform Finally Passed, Health Affairs: Project HOPE, June 1, 2010

22.Jonathan Chait, Conservatives Brace for the Possibility Obamacare Won't Totally Suck, The New Republic, July 23, 2013

23.Tim Cohen, Rough Obamacare rollout: 4 reasons why, CNN, October 2013, https://www.cnn.com/2013/10/22/politics/obamacare-website-four-reasons/index.html

24.Sydney J. Freedberg Jr, The myth of the $600 hammer, Government Executive, December 7, 1998, https://www.govexec.com/federal-news/1998/12/the-myth-of-the-600-hammer/5271/

25.OccupyWallStreet-About, The Occupy Solidarity Network, Inc, Archived July 20, 2014, http://occupywallst.org/about/

26.Intellectual Roots of Wall St. Protest Lie in Academe – Movement's principles arise from scholarship on anarchy, The Chronicle of Higher Education, October 16, 2011

27.Andrew Fleming, Adbusters sparks Wall Street protest Vancouver-based activists behind street actions in the U.S., The Vancouver Courier, September 27, 2011

28.Manuel Valdes, Occupy protests move to foreclosed homes, Yahoo Finance, Archived January 8, 2012, Retrieved July 12, 2012, https://web.archive.org/web/20120109102152/http://finance.yahoo.com/news/occupy-protests-move-foreclosed-homes-222757553.html

29.Robert Weissman, Occupy' Movement Purposely Has No Single Set Demand, US News, October 19, 2011, Archived October 20, 2011,

https://web.archive.org/web/20111020031546/http://www.usnews.com/d
ebate-club/is-occupy-wall-street-the-next-tea-party-movement/occupy-
movement-purposely-has-no-single-set-demand-occupy-movement-
purposely-has-no-single-set-demand
30.Peter Grier, McCain fleshes out his economic plan, Christian Science
Monitor, April 28, 2008, Retrieved May 17, 2008,
http://www.csmonitor.com/2008/0428/p02s02-uspo.html
31.The McCain Budget Plan, The Washington Post, July 14, 2008,
https://www.washingtonpost.com/wp-
dyn/content/article/2008/07/13/AR2008071301643_pf.html
32.John McCain on Free Trade, On the Issues, Retrieved April 18, 2008,
http://www.ontheissues.org/2008/John_McCain_Free_Trade.htm
33.The Voter's Self Defense System, Vote Smart,
http://www.votesmart.org/npat.php?can_id=53270#1062
34.Bill Scher, McCain Lies About Social Security Privatization, Yahoo!News,
Retrieved July 9, 2008,
https://news.yahoo.com/s/huffpost/20080613/cm_huffpost/106862
35.U.S. Senate: U.S. Senate Roll Call Votes 107th Congress – 2nd Session,
www.senate.gov
36.Michael D Shear, McCain Embraces Regulation After Many Years of
Opposition, The Washington Post pp. A01, September 17, 2008,
 https://www.washingtonpost.com/wp-
dyn/content/article/2008/09/16/AR2008091603732_pf.html
37.U.S. Senate: U.S. Senate Roll Call Votes 110th Congress – 1st Session,
www.senate.gov
38.McCain says he supports the minimum wage after voting against it 19
times, Archived September 28, 2008, the Wayback Machine
39.McCain's voting record shows worker issues not his priority, Michigan
Building and Construction Trades Council, May 16, 2008,
https://www.michiganbuildingtrades.org/newspaper/mccains-voting-record-
shows-worker-issues-not-his-priority
40.Ali Zaslav, Clare Foran, Morgan Rimmer, Kristin Wilson, Here are the 19
Republicans who voted for the bipartisan infrastructure bill, CNN Retrieved
2021, 11-06,
 https://www.cnn.com/2021/08/10/politics/republican-senators-voted-
infrastructure-bill/index.html
41.Alexander Bolton, Romney's about face on campaign funding, The Hill,
February 8, 2007,
https://web.archive.org/web/20071118085947/http://thehill.com/leading-
the-news/romneys-about-face-on-campaign-funding-2007-02-08.html
42.Governor hopefuls debate, Sunday Republican, Springfield,
Massachusetts, October 27, 2002

43.Kasie Hunt, Romney would raise Medicare eligibility age, The Guardian, February 24 2012

44.Danny Yadron, Romney, Adjust minimum wage for inflation, The Wall Street Journal Associated Press, February 1, 2012, https://blogs.wsj.com/washwire/2012/02/01/romney-adjust-minimum-wage-for-inflation/

45.Wayne Washington, Glen Johnson, Romney weights in – carefully – on Bush tax-cut plan, Governor won't give his endorsement, The Boston Globe, April 22, 2003

46.CNN late edition with wolf blitzer, CNN, January 4, 2009, https://web.archive.org/web/20120117020415/http://www-cgi.cnn.com/TRANSCRIPTS/0901/04/le.01.html

47.Felicia Somnez, Romney supports 'cut, cap, balance' pledge, The Washington Post, June 29, 2011, https://www.washingtonpost.com/blogs/2chambers/post/romney-supports-cut-cap-balance-pledge/2011/06/29/AGbXD4qH_blog.html

48.Mitt Romney, Regulation: Cutting the red tape, MittRomney.com, July 25, 2012, https://web.archive.org/web/20120725211004/http://www.mittromney.com/issues/regulation

49.Charles Riley, JPMorgan and the politics of financial reform, CNN Money, May 12, 2012, https://money.cnn.com/2012/05/11/news/economy/politics-jpmorgan-regulation/

50.An ad claims Mitt Romney housing policy is to let foreclosures 'hit the bottom', Politifact, November 24, 2011, http://www.politifact.com/truth-o-meter/statements/2011/nov/01/democratic-national-committee/ad-claims-mitt-romneys-housing-policy-let-foreclos/

51.Philip Rucker, Karen Tumulity, Romney unveils sweeping plan for jobs, economy, The Washington Post, September 6, 2011, https://www.washingtonpost.com/politics/romney-to-unveil-plan-for-jobs-economy/2011/09/06/gIQAMUWl6J_story.html

52.Mitt Romney on Trade Policy, The Political Guide, July 13, 2012

53.Stephen Kolf, Obama campaign accuses Mitt Romney of flipping on trade to win Ohio votes, The Plain Dealer, March 1, 2012, http://www.cleveland.com/open/index.ssf/2012/03/obama_campaign_accuses_mitt_ro.html

54.Romney promises 12 million jobs in first term, Yahoo! Finance, Archived August 9, 2012, https://web.archive.org/web/20120809020538/http://finance.yahoo.com/news/romney-promises-12-million-jobs-223400906.html

55.Jacob M. Grumbach, Jacob S. Hacker, Paul Pierson, The Political Economies of Red States, The American Political Economy Politics, Markets, and Power, Cambridge University Press, pp. 209-244

56.Allan Sloan, Cezary Podkul, Donald Trump Built a National Debt So Big (Even Before the Pandemic) That It'll Weigh Down the Economy for Years, ProPublica, January, 14, 2021, https://www.propublica.org/article/national-debt-trump

57.Ken Sweet, Consumers lose chance to sue banks in win for Wall Street, Associated Press, October 25, 2017, https://apnews.com/9121c1b1e4b543aeb9213a60182eb857

58.Melanie Zanona, Trump admin scraps Obama-era proposal requiring airlines to disclose bag fees, The Hill, December 11, 2017, https://thehill.com/policy/transportation/363956-trump-admin-scraps-obama-era-proposal-requiring-airlines-to-disclose

59.Phil McCausland, Trump's proposed SNAP changes could mean millions lose food stamp access, NBC News, November 30, 2019, https://www.nbcnews.com/news/us-news/trump-administration-proposal-could-cause-millions-lose-food-stamps-n1092866

60.Peter Navarro, Wilbur Ross, Scoring the Trump Economic Plan: Trade, Regulatory & Energy Policy Impacts, September 29, 2016, https://web.archive.org/web/20220412025404/https://assets.donaldjtrump.com/Trump_Economic_Plan.pdf

61.Heather Long, Trump has officially put more tariffs on U.S. allies than on China, The Washington Post, May 31, 2018, https://www.washingtonpost.com/news/wonk/wp/2018/05/31/trump-has-officially-put-more-tariffs-on-u-s-allies-than-on-china/

62.Michelle Ye Hee Lee, Donald Trump's claim that China 'will enter' the Trans-Pacific Partnership 'at a later date', The Washington Post, June 30, 2016, https://www.washingtonpost.com/news/fact-checker/wp/2016/06/30/donald-trumps-claim-that-china-will-enter-the-trans-pacific-partnership-at-a-later-date/

63.Thomas Kaplan, Alan Rappeport, Republican Tax Bill Passes Senate in 51-48 Vote, The New York Times, December 19, 2017, https://www.nytimes.com/2017/12/19/us/politics/tax-bill-vote-congress.html

64.Jane C. Timm, Trump signs tax cut bill, first big legislative win, NBC News, December 22, 2017, https://www.nbcnews.com/politics/politics-news/trump-signs-tax-cut-bill-first-big-legislative-win-n832141

65.Dylan Matthews, The numbers are in: Trump's tax plan is a bonanza for the rich, not the middle-class, Vox, https://www.vox.com/policy-and-politics/2017/9/29/16384274/big-six-tax-reform-congress-trump-tax-policy-center

66.Richard Rubin, Treasury Removes Paper at Odds With Mnuchin's Take on Corporate-Tax Cut's Winners, The Wall Street Journal, September 28, 2017

67.Jill Colvin, Trump's plans if he returns to the White House include deportation raids, tariffs and mass firings, AP News, November 12, 2023, https://apnews.com/article/trump-policies-agenda-election-2024-second-term-d656d8f08629a8da14a65c4075545e0f

68.Beverly Gage, More 'Progressive' Than Thou, The New York Times, January, 12, 2016,
 https://www.nytimes.com/2016/01/17/magazine/more-progressive-than-thou.html

69.Elizabeth Warren's critique of Hillary Clinton's 2001 bankruptcy vote, The Washington Post, Retrieved June 5, 2016,
 https://www.washingtonpost.com/news/fact-checker/wp/2016/02/09/elizabeth-warrens-critique-of-hillary-clintons-2001-bankruptcy-vote/

70.Mandi Woodruff, How Hillary Clinton might solve the student debt crisis, Yahoo Finance, May 1, 2015,
 https://finance.yahoo.com/news/how-hillary-clinton-might-solve-the-student-debt-crisis-153633224.html

71.Sam Levine, Hillary Clinton Pledges Constitutional Amendment To Overturn Citizens United in Her First 30 Days, The Huffington Post, July 16, 2016, http://www.huffingtonpost.com/entry/hillary-clinton-citizens-united_us_578a42cfe4b08608d334c7bd

72.Rob Dietz, Klein, Raasch praised Guiliani's misrepresentation of Clinton quote, Media Matters for America, May 18, 2007, http://mediamatters.org/research/2007/05/18/klein-raasch-praised-giulianis-misrepresentatio/138894

73.Tory Newmyer, Hillary Clinton,: Capitalism is out of balance, needs a reset, Fortune, July 24, 2015,
 http://fortune.com/2015/07/24/hillary-says-capitalism-needs-a-reset/

74.Tessa Berenson, Hillary Clinton and Bernie Sanders Spar on Capitalism in First Debate, Time, October 13, 2015,
 http://time.com/4072583/democratic-debate-hillary-clinton-bernie-sanders-capitalism/

75.Amy Chozick, Clinton Offers Economic Plan Focused on Jobs, The New York Times, March 4, 2016,
 https://www.nytimes.com/2016/03/05/us/politics/hillary-clinton-offers-economic-plan-focused-on-jobs.html

76.The enormous ambition of Hillary Clinton's child-care plan, The Washington Post, Retrieved August 3, 2016, https://www.washingtonpost.com/news/wonk/wp/2016/05/12/the-enormous-ambition-of-hillary-clintons-child-care-plan/

77.Lauren Carroll, Hillary Clinton says she called for Wall Street regulations early in the financial crisis, PolitiFact, July 15, 2015, http://www.politifact.com/truth-o-meter/statements/2015/jul/15/hillary-clinton/hillary-clinton-says-she-called-wall-street-regula/

78.2016 Fiscal Fact Check: Adding Up Secretary Clinton's Campaign Proposals So Far, Committee for a Responsible Federal Budget, May 2, 2016, http://fiscalfactcheck.crfb.org/adding-up-secretary-clintons-campaign-proposals-so-far/

79.Sam Frizell, Hillary Clinton's pledge to avoid middle-class tax hikes is bad news for progressive politics, Vox, December 19, 2015, http://time.com/4126685/hillary-clinton-middle-class-tax-pledge/

80.Richard C. Auxier, Leonard E. Burnam, James R. Nunns, Jeffrey Rohaly, Research Report: An Analysis of Hillary Clinton's Tax Proposals, Tax Policy Center, March 3, 2016, http://www.taxpolicycenter.org/publications/analysis-hillary-clintons-tax-proposals

81.Linda Qiu, PolitiFact's guide to the 2016 presidential candidate tax plans, PolitiFact, April 7, 2016, http://www.politifact.com/truth-o-meter/article/2016/apr/07/politifacts-guide-2016-candidates-tax-plans/

82.Aimee Picchi, Why 200 millionaires want higher taxes: Inequality is "eating our world alive", CBSNEWS MoneyWatch, January 18, 2023, https://www.cbsnews.com/news/millionaires-higher-taxes-on-rich-davos-inequality/

83.Lauren Carroll, Does Hillary Clinton want a $15 or $12 minimum wage? PolitiFact, April 15, 2016, http://www.politifact.com/truth-o-meter/statements/2016/apr/15/bernie-s/does-hillary-clinton-want-15-or-12-minimum-wage/

84.Religion and Politics '09: Hillary Clinton, Pew Research Center, November 8, 2008, https://www.pewforum.org/2008/11/04/religion-and-politics-08-hillary-clinton/

85.Hillary Clinton, It's not business that create jobs, USA Today, Retrieved October 27, 2014, http://onpolitics.usatoday.com/2014/10/25/hillary-clinton-its-not-businesses-that-create-jobs/

86.Bernie Sanders joins Hillary Clinton at New Hampshire event, MSNBC, Retrieve July 12, 2016, http://www.msnbc.com/live-online/watch/live-sanders-campaigns-with-clinton-in-nh-723409987752?cid=sm_tw_msnbc

87.Erich Wagner, Biden to Sign Executive Order Killing Schedule F, Restoring Collective Bargaining Rights, Government Executive, January 22, 2021,

https://www.govexec.com/management/2021/01/biden-sign-executive-order-killing-schedule-f-restoring-collective-bargaining-rights/171569/
88.Josh Boak, Biden's executive actions for economic relief at a glance, The Washington Post, January 22, 2021, https://web.archive.org/web/20210130233354/https://www.washingtonpost.com/business/bidens-executive-actions-for-economic-relief-at-a-glance/2021/01/22/fc4f89dc-5cf4-11eb-a849-6f9423a75ffd_story.html
89.Ben Penn, DOL Unwinds Trump Rule That Upped Union Financial Oversight (1), Bloomberg Daily Labor Report & News. Bloomberg Law, March 29, 2021, https://news.bloomberglaw.com/daily-labor-report/dol-unwinds-trump-rule-that-tightened-union-financial-oversight
90.Biden calls on Congress to avert 'national rail shutdown', AP News, November 28, 2022, https://apnews.com/article/business-congress-government-and-politics-44c88740ed57ba96a20c4fc6fffb230b
91.Biden to show solidarity with striking UAW workers in historic move, PBS, September 26, 2023, https://www.pbs.org/newshour/politics/biden-to-show-solidarity-with-striking-uaw-workers-in-historic-move
92.President-elect Biden Announces American Rescue Plan, The White House, January 14, 2021, https://web.archive.org/web/20210123050648/https://buildbackbetter.gov/wp-content/uploads/2021/01/COVID_Relief-Package-Fact-Sheet.pdf
93.Jacob Pramuk, Biden signs $1.9 trillion Covid relief bill, clearing way for stimulus checks, vaccine aid, CNBC, March 11, 2021, https://www.cnbc.com/2021/03/11/biden-1point9-trillion-covid-relief-package-thursday-afternoon.html
94.Jim Tankersley, Biden Will Seek Tax Increase on Rich to Fund Child Care and Education, The New York Times, April 22, 2021
95.Arnie, Seipel, Joe Manchin says he won't support President Biden's Build Back Better plan, NPR, December 19, 2021, https://www.npr.org/2021/12/19/1065636709/joe-manchin-says-he-cannot-support-bidens-build-back-better-plan
96.Fact Sheet: The American Jobs Plan, The White House, March 31, 2021, Retrieved March 31, 2021, https://www.whitehouse.gov/briefing-room/statements-releases/2021/03/31/fact-sheet-the-american-jobs-plan/
97.How Democrats plan to overhaul taxes, climate spending, and health care before the midterms, Vox, July 27, 2022, Retrieved August 24, 2022, https://www.vox.com/23281547/build-back-better-joe-manchin-inflation-reduction-act

98.Rachel Siegel, What's in Biden's $2 trillion jobs and infrastructure plan, The Washington Post, March 31, 2021, Retrieved June 23, 2021, https://www.washingtonpost.com/us-policy/2021/03/31/what-is-in-biden-infrastructure-plan/

99.Ted Gotsch, American Jobs Plan Will Grow the Middle Class, International Brotherhood of Teamsters, April 21, 2021, Retrieved June 23, 2021, https://teamster.org/2021/04/american-jobs-plan-will-grow-the-middle-class/

100.Ella Nilsen, Joe Biden's $2 trillion infrastructure and jobs plan, explained, Vox, March 31, 2021,
 https://www.vox.com/2021/3/31/22357179/biden-two-trillion-infrastructure-jobs-plan-explained

101.Jim Tankersley, Dana Goldstein, Biden Details $1.8 Trillion Plan for Workers, Student and Families, The New York Times, April 28, 2021, Archived April 28, 2021

102.CBO Scores IRA with $238 Billion of Deficit Reduction, Committee for a Responsible Federal Budget, September, 7, 2022, https://www.crfb.org/blogs/cbo-scores-ira-238-billion-deficit-reduction

103.Lorie Konish, How Democratic presidential candidate Joe Biden plans to increase Social Security benefits, CNBC, July 29, 2019, https://www.cnbc.com/2019/07/29/how-joe-biden-plans-to-increase-americas-social-security-benefits.html

104.Jack Caporal, John Hoffner, What is Former Vice President Biden's Policy on Trade? Center for Strategic and International Studies, February 12, 2020, https://www.csis.org/analysis/what-former-vice-president-bidens-policy-trade

105.Andrew Gussert, Biden's Record on Trade, Institute for Agriculture and Trade Policy/Citizens Trade Campaign, September 17, 2008, https://web.archive.org/web/20200823084522/https://www.iatp.org/news/bidens-record-on-trade

106.Mike Lillis, Biden coaxes Dems on Obama trade deal, The Hill, January 28, 2016, https://thehill.com/homenews/house/267420-biden-coaxes-dems-on-obama-trade-deal

107.Joseph R Biden Jr, Why America Must Lead Again, Foreign Affairs, March-April 2020, Retrieved October 6, 2021, https://www.foreignaffairs.com/articles/united-states/2020-01-23/why-america-must-lead-again

108.Ana Swanson, Biden's Commerce Pick Vows to Combat China and Climate Change, The New York Times, January 26, 2021

109.Bob Davis, Yuka Hayashi, New Trade Representative Says U.S. Isn't Ready to Lift China Tariffs, The Wall Street Journal, March 28, 2021

110.The White House, FACT SHEET: Biden-Harris Administration Announces New Private and Public Sector Investments for Affordable Electric Vehicles, Whitehouse.gov, April 17, 2023, https://www.whitehouse.gov/briefing-room/statements-releases/2023/04/17/fact-sheet-biden-harris-administration-announces-new-private-and-public-sector-investments-for-affordable-electric-vehicles

111.Daniel Yergin, The Major Problems Blocking America's Electric Car Future Politico, August 31, 2021, https://www.politico.com/news/magazine/2021/08/31/biden-electric-vehicles-problems-yergin-507599

112.Trina Paul, Why is inflation so high? An economist explains why everyday essentials cost more, CNBC, August 15, 2023, https://www.cnbc.com/select/why-is-inflation-so-high/

113.Ben S. Bernanke, Olivier Blanchard, What cause the U.S. pandemic-era inflation?, brookings.edu, June 13, 2023, https://www.brookings.edu/articles/what-caused-the-u-s-pandemic-era-inflation/

114.Preston Caldwell, Why We Expect Inflation to Fall in 2023, Morningstar.com, October 12, 2023, https://www.morningstar.com/economy/why-we-expect-inflation-fall-2023-2

115.PBS, WATCH: Biden says he's helped lower inflation during the first meeting of his new supply chain council, PBS, November 27, 2023, https://www.pbs.org/newshour/politics/watch-live-biden-speaks-on-efforts-to-improve-supply-chains-and-lower-inflation

116.Ballotpedia, Dean Phillips presidential campaign, 2024, Ballotpedia, Retrieved November 29, 2023, https://ballotpedia.org/Dean_Phillips_presidential_campaign,_2024

117.Ballotpedia, Marianne Williamson presidential campaign, 2024, Ballotpedia, Retrieved November 29, 2023, https://ballotpedia.org/Marianne_Williamson_presidential_campaign,_2024

118.Marianne Williamson, An Economic Bill of Rights: A Vision for a Moral Economy, Retrieved November 29, 2023, https://marianne2024.com/economic-bill-of-rights/

119.Ballotpedia, Ryan Binkley presidential campaign, 2024, Ballotpedia, Retrieved November 29, 2023, https://ballotpedia.org/Ryan_Binkley_presidential_campaign,_2024

120.Ballotpedia, Doug Burgum presidential campaign, 2024, Ballotpedia, Retrieved November 29, 2023, https://ballotpedia.org/Doug_Burgum_presidential_campaign,_2024

121.Ballotpedia, Chris Christie presidential campaign, 2024, Ballotpedia, Retrieved November 29, 2023, https://ballotpedia.org/Chris_Christie_(New_Jersey)

122.Ballotpedia, Ron DeSantis presidential campaign, 2024, Ballotpedia, Retrieved November 29, 2023, https://ballotpedia.org/Ron_DeSantis_presidential_campaign,_2024

123.Tammy Luhby, Here's what's in DeSantis' economic plan, CNN Politics, August 1, 2023, https://www.cnn.com/2023/08/01/politics/ron-desantis-economic-plan-president/index.html

124.Ballotpedia, Nikki Haley presidential campaign, 2024, Ballotpedia, Retrieved November 29, 2023, https://ballotpedia.org/Nikki_Haley_presidential_campaign,_2024

125.Ebony Davis, Nikki Haley unveils economic proposal while slamming both parties over government spending, CNN Politics, September 22, 2023, https://www.cnn.com/2023/09/22/politics/nikki-haley-economic-proposal/index.html

126.Ballotpedia, Asa Hutchinson presidential campaign, 2024, Ballotpedia, Retrieved November 29, 2023, https://ballotpedia.org/Asa_Hutchinson_presidential_campaign,_2024

127.Ballotpedia, Vivek Ramaswamy presidential campaign, 2024, Ballotpedia, Retrieved November 29, 2023, https://ballotpedia.org/Vivek_Ramaswamy_presidential_campaign,_2024

128.Ballotpedia, Cornel West presidential campaign, 2024, Ballotpedia, Retrieved November 29, 2023, https://ballotpedia.org/Cornel_West

129.Ballotpedia, Jill Stein presidential campaign, 2024, Ballotpedia, Retrieved November 29, 2023, https://ballotpedia.org/Jill_Stein

130.Emma Nicholson, Annie Bryson, Jill Stein announces 2024 presidential bid as Green Party candidate, CBS News, November 10, 2023, https://www.cbsnews.com/news/jill-stein-green-party-2024-presidential-bid/

131.Ballotpedia, Chase Oliver presidential campaign, 2024, Ballotpedia, Retrieved November 29, 2023, https://ballotpedia.org/Chase_Oliver

132.Ballotpedia, Robert F. Kennedy, Jr. presidential campaign, 2024, Ballotpedia, Retrieved November 29, 2023, https://ballotpedia.org/Robert_F._Kennedy_Jr.

133.Michael Bernick, Labor Day 2023: Bobby Kennedy's Heterodox Jobs Plans, Forbes, August 22, 2023, https://www.forbes.com/sites/michaelbernick/2023/08/22/labor-day-2023-bobby-kennedys-heterodox-jobs-plan/?sh=4bf0da2c1ebc

134.Rachel Frazin, Harris: 'I am not a socialist', The Hill, November 23, 2019, https://thehill.com/policy/finance/471802-harris-i-am-not-a-socialist

135.Lauren Feiner, Warren and Harris introduce Senate bill to crack down on price gouging during the coronavirus pandemic, CNBC, April 10, 2020, https://www.cnbc.com/2020/04/10/coronavirus-price-gouging-bill-from-warren-fights-price-gouging.html

136.	Zack Budryk, Kamala Harris says she wouldn't have voted for NAFTA, The Hill, May 12, 2019, https://thehill.com/homenews/campaign/443314-kamala-harris-says-she-wouldnt-have-voted-for-nafta

137.David Weigel, Sen. Kamala Harris backs Bernie Sanders' single-payer bill, The Washington Post, August 30, 2017, https://www.washingtonpost.com/news/powerpost/wp/2017/08/31/sen-kamala-harris-backs-bernie-sanderss-single-payer-bill/

138.Jeff Stein, Analysis: Almost all of Sen. Harris' $2.8 trillion tax plan would help middle and working class, study finds, The Washington Post, November 15, 2018, https://www.washingtonpost.com/business/2018/11/15/almost-all-sen-harriss-trillion-tax-plan-would-help-middle-working-class-study-finds/

139.John Whitesides, Amanda Becker, Democratic U.S. Sen Kamala Harris Jumps into 2020 White House Race, Reuters, January 21, 2019, https://www.reuters.com/article/us-usa-election-harris-idUSKCN1PF16J

140.Alex Woodward, The Pandemic has been an accelerator: Kamala Harris joines Bernie Sanders in campaign for minimum wage hike, Independent UK, October 30, 2020, https://www.independent.co.uk/news/world/americas/us-election-2020/joe-biden-minimum-wage-kamala-harris-bernie-sanders-us-election-2020-b1437214.html

CHAPTER EIGHT

1.Pub. L. 75-718, ch. 676, 52 Stat 1060, June 25, 1938
2.WHD U.S. Wage and Hour Division, The Fair Labor Standards Act of 1938, As Amended, U.S. Department of Labor, Wage and Hour Division, WH Publication 1318, Revised May 2011,
https://www.dol.gov/sites/dolgov/files/WHD/legacy/files/FairLaborStand Act.pdf
3.Library of Congress, The Industrial Revolution in the United States, Library of Congress Archives,
  https://www.loc.gov/classroom-materials/industrial-revolution-in-the-united-states/
4.U.S. Department of Labor, History of Federal Minimum Wage Rates Under the Fair Labor Standards Act, 1938 - 2009,
https://www.dol.gov/agencies/whd/minimum-wage/history/chart
5.Aimee Picchi, Most middle-class American say they can't support their cost of living, survey finds, CBS News Money Watch, July 20, 2022,
https://www.cbsnews.com/news/inflation-75-percent-of-middle-class-americans-say-income-below-cost-of-living/
6.Adam Hayes, Does Raising the Minimum Wage Increase Inflation?, May 30, 2023,
  https://www.investopedia.com/ask/answers/052815/does-raising-minimum-wage-increase-inflation.asp
7.Raisa Bruner, The Great Resignation Fueled Higher Pay—Even For Those Who Didn't Switch Jobs, TIME, January 27, 2022,
https://time.com/6143212/us-wage-growth-record-high/
8.Scott Horsley, Inflation has cooled a lot. So why do things still feel so expensive?, NPR, December 16, 2023,
  https://www.npr.org/2023/12/16/1219574403/economy-inflation-prices-wages-disinflation-deflation-interest-rates
9.U.S. Department of Labor, Wage and Hour Division, Consolidated Minimum Wage Table (By State), U.S. Department of Labor, Retrieved January 11, 2024,
  https://www.dol.gov/agencies/whd/mw-consolidated
10.Janos Allenbach-Ammann, EU Parliament approves Minimum Wage Directive, Euractiv, September 14, 2022,
https://www.euractiv.com/section/economy-jobs/news/eu-parliament-approves-minimum-wage-directive/
11.Dora Katalin Sari, The new EU Directive on minimum wage sets a dual goal, International Labour Organization, November 16, 2022,
  https://www.ilo.org/global/about-the-ilo/newsroom/news/WCMS_861051/lang--en/index.htm

12.EuroDev, Minimum Wage in Europe 2022, EuroDev, June 1, 2023, https://www.eurodev.com/blog/minimum-wage-in-europe-2022

13.Julie Norwell, Working Standards: U.S. vs. Europe, Barrett Group, Career Change, November 7, 2021,
 https://www.careerchange.com/newsletters/working-standards-u-s-vs-europe/

14.Jennifer Liu, All the U.S. states, cities, and countries where companies have to share salary ranges with workers, CNBC, January 3, 2023, https://www.cnbc.com/2023/01/03/where-us-companies-have-to-share-salary-ranges-with-workers-by-law.html

15.INS Global, How To Safely Terminate Employment in Europe, INSGLOBAL, March 31, 2023,
 https://ins-globalconsulting.com/news-post/terminate-employment-europe/

16.Kensington Additive, The 7 Key Differences Between Working In The US and EU, Kensington Additive, Retrieved January 15, 2024, https://www.kensingtonadditive.co.uk/blog/2021/09/the-7-key-differences-between-working-in-the-us-and-eu-in-additive-manufacturing?source=google.com

17.Department of Labor, WARN Act Compliance Assistance, U.S. Department of Labor, Retrieved January 15, 2024,
 https://www.dol.gov/agencies/eta/layoffs/warn

18.Michael Moore, Roger & Me, film, 1989

19.Joseph Thorndike, Reagan's Tax Cut Just Turned 40 — And It's Still The Most Important Tax Reform Since World War II, Forbes, September 3, 2021,
 https://www.forbes.com/sites/taxnotes/2021/09/03/reagans-tax-cut-just-turned-40---and-its-still-the-most-important-tax-reform-since-world-war-ii/?sh=43e2fd225d14

20.Emily Horton, The Legacy of the 2001 and 2003 "Bush" Tax Cuts, Center on Budget and Policy Priorities, October 23, 2017, https://www.cbpp.org/research/the-legacy-of-the-2001-and-2003-bush-tax-cuts

21.Jane C. Timm, Trump signs tax cut bill, first big legislative win, NBC News, December 22, 2017,
 https://www.nbcnews.com/politics/politics-news/trump-signs-tax-cut-bill-first-big-legislative-win-n832141

22.IRS Revenue Procedures, Highest Income Brackets, TaxPolicyCenter.org, May 22, 2003,
 https://www.taxpolicycenter.org/statistics/historical-highest-marginal-income-tax-rates

23.Christopher S. Rugaber, Study: Obama tax hikes on rich didn't hurt economy, or rich, AP News, November 3, 2016,

https://apnews.com/article/87553d69f3294e1fb3d0a5912f2e6e31
24.Julia Kagan, Bush Tax Cuts: What They are, How They Work, Downside, Investopedia, August 9, 2022,
 https://www.investopedia.com/terms/b/bush-tax-cuts.asp
25.IRS, Current Capital Gains Tax Rates, Internal Revenue Service Center, Retrieved January 16, 2024,
 https://www.irs.gov/taxtopics/tc409
26.Will Kenton, Reagonomics: Definition, Policies, and Impact, Investopedia, January 10, 2023,
 https://www.investopedia.com/terms/r/reaganomics.asp
27.David Floyd, Explaining the Trump Tax Reform Plan, Investopedia, January 23, 2023,
https://www.investopedia.com/taxes/trumps-tax-reform-plan-explained/
28.Seth Hanlon and Nick Buffle, The Forbes 400 Pay Lower Tax Rates Than Many Ordinary American, American Progress, October 7, 2021,
https://www.americanprogress.org/article/forbes-400-pay-lower-tax-rates-many-ordinary-americans/
29.John Stuart Mill, Utilitarianism, London, Parker, Son & Bourn, West Strand, 1863
30.Andrew Bloomenthal, Marginal Utilities: Definition, Types, Examples, and History, Investopedia, December 19, 2023,
https://www.investopedia.com/terms/m/marginalutility.asp
31.Julie Young, Too Big to Fail: Definition, History, and Reforms, Investopedia, November 13, 2023,
 https://www.investopedia.com/terms/t/too-big-to-fail.asp
32.Center on Budget and Policy Priorities, Policy Basics: The Earned Income Tax Credit, Center on Budget and Policy Priorities, April 28, 2023,
https://www.cbpp.org/research/policy-basics-the-earned-income-tax-credit
33.Adam Hayes, What Is a Loss Carryback? Definition, History, and Example, Investopedia, July 24, 2022,
 https://www.investopedia.com/terms/l/losscarryback.asp
34.Jim Probasco, Alternative Minimum Tax (AMT) Definition, How It Works, Investopedia, January 2, 2023,
 https://www.investopedia.com/terms/a/alternativeminimumtax.asp
35.Danielle Kurtzleben, FACT CHECK: Does The U.S. Have The Highest Corporate Tax Rate In The World?, NPR, August 7, 2017,
https://www.npr.org/2017/08/07/541797699/fact-check-does-the-u-s-have-the-highest-corporate-tax-rate-in-the-world
36.Price Waterhouse, Canada – Corporate – Other Taxes, PWC-Price Waterhouse, Retrieved January 16, 2024,
https://taxsummaries.pwc.com/canada/corporate/other-taxes

37.Stephen C. Goss, The Future Financial Status of the Social Security Program, Social Security, Office of Retirement and Disability Policy, Social Security Bulletin, Vol 70, November 3, 2010, Retrieved January 17, 2024, https://www.ssa.gov/policy/docs/ssb/v70n3/v70n3p111.html

38.James McWhinney, The Demise of the Defined-Benefit Plan and What Replaced It, Investopedia, November 19, 2023, https://www.investopedia.com/articles/retirement/06/demiseofdbplan.asp

39.Komaron McNair, 56% of Americans say they're not on track to comfortably retire—how to catch up, CNBC, September 8, 2023, https://www.cnbc.com/2023/09/08/56percent-of-americans-say-theyre-not-on-track-to-comfortably-retire.html

40.Peter G. Peterson Foundation, Interest Costs On The National Debt Are On Track To Reach A Record High, Peter G. Peterson Foundation, February 16, 2023, https://www.pgpf.org/blog/2023/02/interest-costs-on-the-national-debt-are-on-track-to-reach-a-record-high

41.Paul Constant, Only in America is filing taxes such a complicated mess. Here's how other countries do it better., Business Insider, August 14, 2021, https://www.businessinsider.com/filing-taxes-america-system-how-other-countries-do-better-2021-8

42.MacKenzie Behm, Some Countries Do Your Taxes For You. Here's Why the US Doesn't, LX Home, April 8, 2022, https://www.lx.com/money/some-countries-do-your-taxes-for-you-heres-why-the-us-doesnt/51300/

43.The Commonwealth Fund, U.S. Health Care from a Global Perspective, 2022: Accelerating Spending, Worsening Outcomes, The Commonwealth Fund, Issue Brief, January 31, 2023, https://www.commonwealthfund.org/publications/issue-briefs/2023/jan/us-health-care-global-perspective-2022

44.Lorie Konish, 137 million Americans are struggling with medical debt. Here's what to know if you need some relief, CNBC, November 10, 2019, https://www.cnbc.com/2019/11/10/americans-are-drowning-in-medical-debt-what-to-know-if-you-need-help.html

45.Healthcare.gov, Medicaid expansion and what it means for you, healthcare.gov, Retrieved January 17, 2024, https://www.healthcare.gov/medicaid-chip/medicaid-expansion-and-you/

46.Betsy Reed, A ticking time bomb: healthcare under threat across western Europe, The Guardian, Retrieved January 17, 2024, https://www.theguardian.com/society/2022/dec/14/a-ticking-time-bomb-healthcare-under-threat-across-western-europe

47.Lisa Goetz, 6 European Countries With Free College Tuition, Investopedia, August 5, 2023, https://www.investopedia.com/articles/personal-finance/080616/6-countries-virtually-free-college-tuition.asp

48.Thom Hartman, Student Loan Debt Is an American Malignancy Born of Ronald Reagan, Common Dreams, August 26, 2022, https://www.commondreams.org/views/2022/08/26/student-loan-debt-american-malignancy-born-ronald-reagan

49.Chart, Economic Policy Institute, Wages of young college grads have been falling since 2000, Retrieved January 17, 2024, https://www.epi.org/publication/charting-wage-stagnation/

50.University of the People, Is Tuition-Free Education a Possibility in the USA?, University of the People, Retrieved January 17, 2024, https://www.uopeople.edu/blog/the-history-of-tuition-free-education-in-the-u-s-a/

51.Thomas Adam, College Was Once Free and For the Public Good—What Happened?, Yes Magazine, July 20, 2017, https://www.yesmagazine.org/economy/2017/07/20/college-was-once-free-and-for-the-public-good-what-happened

52.Michael Stone, What Happened When American States Tried Providing Tuition-Free College, TIME, April 4, 2016, https://time.com/4276222/free-college/

53.Jessica Bryant, John Boitnott, Why Is College So Expensive? 5 Reasons, bestcolleges.com, October 12, 2023, https://www.bestcolleges.com/news/analysis/why-is-college-so-expensive/

54.Robin Hartill, Katie Lowery, Andrew Pentis, Why is college so expensive?, CNN Underscored Money, November 10, 2023, https://www.cnn.com/cnn-underscored/money/why-is-college-so-expensive

55.Hanneh Bareham, Why is college so expensive?, bankrate.com, March 27, 2023, https://www.bankrate.com/loans/student-loans/why-is-college-expensive/

56.Preston Cooper, A New Study Investigates Why College Tuition Is So Expensive, Forbes, August 31, 2020, https://www.forbes.com/sites/prestoncooper2/2020/08/31/a-new-study-investigates-why-college-tuition-is-so-expensive/?sh=3a1d8ab717a0

57.David Schaper, Potholes, Grid Failures, Aging Tunnels And Bridges: Infrastructure Gets A C-Minus, NPR, March 3, 2021, https://www.npr.org/2021/03/03/973054080/potholes-grid-failures-aging-tunnels-and-bridges-nations-infrastructure-gets-a-c

58.Renee Valdes, How Long Does It Take To Charge An Electric Car?, Kelley Blue Book, July 11, 2023, https://www.kbb.com/car-advice/how-long-does-take-charge-electric-car/

59.CBC News, Electric vehicles lose up to 30% range when temperatures dip below freezing, study finds, CBC News, February 7, 2023, https://www.cbc.ca/news/canada/sudbury/electric-vehicle-cold-range-1.6738892

60.Tam Harbert, Here's how much the 2008 bailouts really cost, MIT Management Sloan School, February 21, 2019, https://mitsloan.mit.edu/ideas-made-to-matter/heres-how-much-2008-bailouts-really-cost

61.Alex Lach, 5 Facts About Overseas Outsourcing, American Progress.org, July 9, 2012, https://www.americanprogress.org/article/5-facts-about-overseas-outsourcing/

62.Robert Reich, Hillary and Barack, Afta Nafta, Robert Reich.org, February 29, 2008, https://robertreich.org/post/257309371

63.Robert Reich, Robert Reich: Trade agreements are simply ravaging the middle class, Salon.com, March 16, 2016, https://www.salon.com/2016/03/16/robert_reich_trade_deals_are_gutting_the_middle_class_partner/

64.Andrew Beattie, A History of U.S. Monopolies, Investopedia, September 11, 2022, https://www.investopedia.com/insights/history-of-us-monopolies/

65.Environmental Protection Agency, Biden-Harris Administration Finalizes Standards to Slash Methane Pollution, Combat Climate Change, Protect Health, and Bolster American Innovation, EPA.gov, December 2, 2023, https://www.epa.gov/newsreleases/biden-harris-administration-finalizes-standards-slash-methane-pollution-combat-climate

66.Miranda Willson, Heather Richards, Brian Dabbs, Biden regulatory plan set to shake up energy sector, E&E News Energy Wire, December 7, 2023, https://www.eenews.net/articles/biden-regulatory-plan-set-to-shake-up-energy-sector/

67.Jim Watson, Biden Makes Sweeping Changes to Oil and Gas Policy, Center for Strategic & International Studies, January 28, 2021 , https://www.csis.org/analysis/biden-makes-sweeping-changes-oil-and-gas-policy

68.Arit John, Big Gulps Safe After New York City Loses Final Appeal to Ban Large Sodas, The Atlantic, July 26, 2014, https://www.theatlantic.com/politics/archive/2014/06/big-gulps-safe-after-new-york-city-loses-final-appeal-to-ban-large-sodas/373508/

69.Julia Kagan, Pigovian Tax: Definition, Purpose, Calculation, and Examples, Investopedia, August 17, 2023, https://www.investopedia.com/terms/p/pigoviantax.asp

70.Leslie A. Perlow, Constance Noonan Hadley, Eunice Eun, Stop the Meeting Madness, Harvard Business Review, July-August 2017, https://hbr.org/2017/07/stop-the-meeting-madness

71.Andrea Hsu, Biden wants federal workforce to come to the office more. Some ask why?, NPR, September 7, 2023, https://www.npr.org/2023/09/07/1196787623/federal-workers-remote-office-ordered-taxpayers-telework-science

72.Morgan Smith, 90% of companies say they'll return to the office by the end of 2024—but the 5-day commute is 'dead,' experts say, CNBC, September 11, 2023, https://www.cnbc.com/2023/09/11/90percent-of-companies-say-theyll-return-to-the-office-by-the-end-of-2024.html

73.Bernard Marr, Warning: Here's Why KPIs Go Wrong So Often, LinkedIn, August 16, 2014, https://www.linkedin.com/pulse/20140816153450-64875646-warning-here-s-why-kpis-go-wrong-so-often

74.JP Morgan Chase, Small businesses are an anchor of the US economy, JP Morgan Chase, Retrieved January 24, 2024, https://www.jpmorganchase.com/institute/research/small-business/small-business-dashboard/economic-activity

75.Steve Milano, Role of Government in Promoting Small Business, smallbusiness.chron.com, January 25, 2019, https://smallbusiness.chron.com/role-government-promoting-small-business-60657.html

CHAPTER NINE

1.Allan Sloan, Cezary Podkul, Donald Trump Built a National Debt So Big (Even Before the Pandemic) That It'll Weigh Down the Economy for Years, ProPublica, January, 14, 2021,
 https://www.propublica.org/article/national-debt-trump
2.U.S. Customs and Border Protection, North American Free Trade Agreement, June 23, 2023, https://www.cbp.gov/trade/north-american-free-trade-agreement
3.Peter B Levy, Encyclopedia of the Clinton Presidency, Greenwood Publishing Group, p.57
4.Andrea Hsu, Biden wants federal workforce to come to the office more. Some ask why?, NPR, September 7, 2023,
 https://www.npr.org/2023/09/07/1196787623/federal-workers-remote-office-ordered-taxpayers-telework-science
5.Miranda Willson, Heather Richards, Brian Dabbs, Biden regulatory plan set to shake up energy sector, E&E News Energy Wire, December 7, 2023,
 https://www.eenews.net/articles/biden-regulatory-plan-set-to-shake-up-energy-sector/
6.Pew Research Center, REPUBLICAN GAINS IN 2022 MIDTERMS DRIVEN MOSTLY BY TURNOUT ADVANTAGE, Pew Research Center, July 12, 2023,
 https://www.pewresearch.org/politics/2023/07/12/voter-turnout-2018-2022/
7.U.S. Department of Labor, Wage and Hour Division, Consolidated Minimum Wage Table (By State), U.S. Department of Labor, Retrieved January 11, 2024,
 https://www.dol.gov/agencies/whd/mw-consolidated
8.Michael Levy, United States presidential election of 2000, Britannica, January 5, 2024,
 https://www.britannica.com/event/United-States-presidential-election-of-2000
9.David C Beckwith, United States presidential election of 2016, Britannica, January 10, 2024,
 https://www.britannica.com/topic/United-States-presidential-election-of-2016/Conventions
10.National Archives, What is the Electoral College?, National Archives, Retrieved February 23, 2024,
 https://www.archives.gov/electoral-college/about
11.Alexis de Tocqueville, Democracy in America, Tocqueville, Alexis De, and Henry Reeve. Democracy in America, .ed by Spencer, John C New York, J. & H.G. Langley, 1845.

12.The White House, The Constitution, The White House, Retrieved February 28, 2024, https://www.whitehouse.gov/about-the-white-house/our-government/the-constitution/

13.United States Senate, About Parties and Leadership | Historical Overview, United States Senate, Retrieved March 5, 2024, https://www.senate.gov/about/origins-foundations/parties-leadership/overview.htm

14.Drew DeSilver, The polarization in today's Congress has roots that go back decades, Pew Research Center, March 10, 2022, https://www.pewresearch.org/short-reads/2022/03/10/the-polarization-in-todays-congress-has-roots-that-go-back-decades/

15.ballotpedia, Ranked-choice voting (RCV), ballotpedia, Retrieved March 5, 2024, https://ballotpedia.org/Ranked-choice_voting_(RCV)

16.Jeffrey M. Jones, Independent Party ID Tied for High; Democratic ID at New Low, GALLUP, January 12, 2024, https://news.gallup.com/poll/548459/independent-party-tied-high-democratic-new-low.aspx

17.Oleksandra Mamchii, Political Parties in the UK, Conservatives to Regional Parties, Best Diplomats, November 20, 2023, https://bestdiplomats.org/political-parties-in-the-uk/

18.National Volunteer Fire Council, Guide to Communicating with Elected Officials, 2018, https://www.nvfc.org/wp-content/uploads/2015/10/ElectedGuide.pdf

19.National Conference of State Legislatures, Recall of State Officials, NCSL, September 15, 2021, https://www.ncsl.org/elections-and-campaigns/recall-of-state-officials

20.USA.GOV, How federal impeachment works, USA.GOV, February 2, 2024, https://www.usa.gov/impeachment

21.Constitution Annotated, Twenty-Fifth Amendment, Constitution Annotated, Retrieved March 5, 2024, https://constitution.congress.gov/constitution/amendment-25/

22.MLA. Alinsky, Saul D., 1909-1972. Rules for Radicals : a Practical Primer for Realistic Radicals. New York :Vintage Books, 1972., https://www.brainyquote.com/quotes/saul_alinsky_745523

23.Andrea Hsu, UAW has a unique strike strategy. It keeps Detroit Big 3 automakers guessing, NPR, September 19, 2023, https://www.npr.org/2023/09/19/1200198072/uaw-strikes-strategy-shawn-fain-labor-big-3-detroit

24.Michael Levitin, Occupy Wall Street Did More Than You Think, The Atlantic, September 14, 2021, https://www.theatlantic.com/ideas/archive/2021/09/how-occupy-wall-street-reshaped-america/620064/

25.Benjamin Franklin Quotes. (n.d.). BrainyQuote.com. Retrieved March 8, 2024, from BrainyQuote.com Web site: https://www.brainyquote.com/quotes/benjamin_franklin_151597

26.Guy Reichard, Dev Murphy, Wiki How: Persuade Someone, Wiki How, June 17, 2023, https://www.wikihow.com/Persuade-Someone

27.Chris Drew, PhD,16 Cancel Culture Examples, helpfulprofessor.com, July 16, 2023, https://helpfulprofessor.com/cancel-culture-examples/

28.Joe Hernandez, A woman is suing McDonald's after being burned by hot coffee. It's not the first time, NPR, September 28, 2023, https://www.npr.org/2023/09/28/1201421914/a-woman-is-suing-mcdonalds-after-being-burned-by-hot-coffee-its-not-the-first-ti

29.Michael Moore, Roger & Me, film, 1989

30.National Labor Relations Board, Your Rights during Union Organizing, National Labor Relations Board, Retrieved March 8 2024, https://www.nlrb.gov/about-nlrb/rights-we-protect/the-law/employees/your-rights-during-union-organizing

31.Jeffrey Fermin, Erin McClure, Wiki How: How to Unionize Your Workplace in 8 Easy Steps, Wiki How, October 27, 2023, https://www.wikihow.com/Unionize-Your-Workplace

32.UFCW, Want to Start a Union at Your Workplace?, UFCW, Retrieved March 8, 2024, https://www.ufcw.org/start-a-union/

33.Worker.gov, Forming a union at a non-union workplace, Worker.gov, Retrieved March 8, 2024, https://www.worker.gov/form-a-union/

AFTERWORD

1.U.S. Department of Labor, Summary of the Major Laws of the Department of Labor, U.S. Department of Labor, Retrieved March 19, 2024, https://www.dol.gov/general/aboutdol/majorlaws

2.James Chen, What Is an Exempt Employee in the Workplace? Pros & Cons, Investopedia, January 23, 2023, https://www.investopedia.com/terms/e/exempt-employee.asp

3.Internal Revenue Service, Independent contractor (self-employed) or employee?, IRS.gov, Retrieved March 19, 2024, https://www.irs.gov/businesses/small-businesses-self-employed/independent-contractor-self-employed-or-employee

4.Jennifer Post, Contract Workers vs. Employees: What Your Business Needs to Know, Business News Daily, November 20, 2023, https://www.businessnewsdaily.com/770-contract-vs-employees-what-you-need-to-know.html

5.U.S. Department of Labor, Continuation of Health Coverage (COBRA), U.S. Department of Labor, Retrieved March 19, 2024, https://www.dol.gov/general/topic/health-plans/cobra

6.Internal Revenue Service, Affordable Care Act Tax Provisions for Employers, IRS.gov, Retrieved March 19, 2024, https://www.irs.gov/affordable-care-act/employers

7.U.S. Department of Labor, Family and Medical Leave (FMLA), U.S. Department of Labor, Retrieved March 20, 2024, https://www.dol.gov/general/topic/benefits-leave/fmla

8.Occupational Safety and Health Administration, OSHA Worker Rights and Protections, OSHA, Retrieved March 20, 2024, https://www.osha.gov/workers

9.Jeffrey Johnson, J.D., Workers' Compensation Laws By State (2024 Guide), Forbes Advisor, November 21, 2022, https://www.forbes.com/advisor/legal/workers-comp/workers-compensation-laws/

10.U.S. Department of Labor, Workers' Compensation, U.S. Department of Labor, Retrieved March 20, 2024, https://www.dol.gov/general/topic/workcomp

11.USA.GOV, Wrongful termination ,USA.GOV, Retrieved March 20, 2024, https://www.usa.gov/wrongful-termination

12.USA.GOV, Discrimination, harassment, and retaliation ,USA.GOV, Retrieved March 20, 2024, https://www.usa.gov/job-discrimination-harassment

13.elaws Advisor, WARN Advisor, Constructive Discharge, U.S. Department of Labor, Retrieved March 20, 2024,

https://webapps.dol.gov/elaws/eta/warn/glossary.asp?p=Constructive%20
Discharge

14.Legal Information Institute, constructive discharge, Cornell Law School,
Retrieved March 20, 2024,
https://www.law.cornell.edu/wex/constructive_discharge

ABOUT THE AUTHOR

Roy Wells has been working as a financial analyst for several decades. He lives in North Carolina with his wonderful wife.